PAPER · 291

CONTENTS

Understanding Contemporary International Arms Transfers

INTRODUCTION

This paper is concerned with the proliferation of conventional weapons. The very concept itself needs an explanation. Why be concerned with the spread of conventional arms and their means of manufacture? If states have a legitimate right to procure arms which contribute to their national security, surely there can be no objection to more-or-less unrestrained weapons sales? But such a *laissez-faire* attitude to arms transfers is increasingly anachronistic in a world characterised by the breakdown of Cold War barriers, the resurgence of ethnic and religious conflicts, and the absence of legitimate means for resolving inter-state disputes. In any case, the spread of ballistic and cruise missiles has begun to affect directly the interests (and territory) of developed Western nations. Their defence policies will increasingly reflect the new threats posed by Third World nations. The fact that arms suppliers themselves are creating some of these threats does nothing to negate the increasing importance of conventional arms flows in undermining a stable world order. Parallel trends in the proliferation of weapons of mass destruction mean that a less manageable international environment may cause significant difficulties for all states in the not too distant future.

A combination of two factors is creating this new situation: the historical legacy of four decades of Cold War arms transfers; and the diminishing technology advantages of developed countries over developing states. In the case of the former, the Cold War fostered the development of large defence industries in each of the major Western states. The same was true in the Soviet Union, and among its allies in the Warsaw Treaty Organisation (WTO). Complex defence trade links were built up within each of the major alliances. These links underlined the supremacy of the bloc leaders (the United States and the Soviet Union) in weapons technology innovation, and distributed technical spin-offs in weapons and dual-use technologies among the respective allies through co-production arrangements. Over four decades these relationships created a large capacity for weapons production, one that routinely exceeded domestic defence requirements.

3

Exploitation of export markets provided a means for Western European arms manufacturers to fulfil excess production capacity, and to sell less advanced versions of cutting-edge weaponry. Developing nations received arms, frequently also political support from one (or sometimes both) of the major blocs, and technical assistance which to some degree met their developmental aspirations. The 'long peace' of the Cold War saw the establishment of stable supplier–recipient relationships, with predictable modes of arms and technology transfer. In turn, political relations between supplier and recipient ensured the one-way (for suppliers) transparency of Third World weapons holdings. The system operated to the benefit of arms producers, and sustained long-term advantages in weapons technology and military capability for developed states.

The end of the Cold War undermined this stable arms-transfer system. The arms market shrank, leaving defence industries in the two blocs with unprecedented levels of excess capacity. The budget deficits of most of the leading weapons-producing nations meant that they were increasingly unwilling to subsidise defence production or research and development (R&D). Supplier governments encouraged their defence firms to seek foreign markets in order to maintain a profitable scale of production. The end of the Cold War also saw the removal of subsidies by suppliers to developing countries which had enabled them to purchase arms they might otherwise have been unable to afford. This has left supplier nations with a severe problem. Domestic markets are now in steep decline. Foreign markets are increasingly competitive, with importers who possess hard currency driving harder bargains in arms-transfer agreements. The buyers' market for arms has altered the terms of trade in the international defence sector.

Purchasers are no longer satisfied with marginal offset benefits but are now insisting on formal offset and technology transfer commitments *prior* to the conclusion of an arms-transfer agreement. In addition, competition among suppliers has led to an escalation in the technology content of transferred weapons. States no longer save their most advanced weapons for their own forces; instead, weapons are appearing on the global market prior to their integration into the leading suppliers' national arsenals. Thus, technology transfer in the arms trade is accelerating, and normal technology security restrictions are under pressure from supply-side competition.

Because technology transfers in the defence trade increasingly foster industrial development in recipient states, indirect and direct offset benefits are creating new arms-manufacturing capacities. This, in turn, is expanding the transnational trade in weapons subcomponents. The spread of arms production also creates new sources for subcomponent technologies, which, if integrated correctly, can increase the effectiveness of transferred weapons. Where these trends affect areas of conflict or tension, they can trigger arms races and the proliferation of weapons in pursuit of short-term advantage.

Specific weapons proliferation trends in cruise and ballistic missiles, or in advanced combat aircraft, can provide delivery vehicles for weapons of mass destruction. This has begun to attract the attention of supplier governments, even those most committed to aggressive exploitation of export markets. What is the correct approach to these increasingly serious trends? How can conventional weapons proliferation be reconciled with arms-export policies which militate against any form of unilateral (or multilateral) restraint? Supply-side strategies, centred in the conflicting interests of the major suppliers, are unlikely to succeed through appeals to morality or to 'world order' interests such as non-proliferation alone. There is no strong international norm against conventional arm sales. In the absence of such a moral precept, those interested in seeing limits placed on conventional arms transfers are left with little alternative but to attempt to stabilise the current situation before it goes beyond multilateral control. Increasing the transparency of the international arms trade, alongside meaningful confidence-building measures in dual-use trade, may provide the basis for progress in this direction.

Beyond these measures, however, the way forward is not obvious. There is no substitute for political leadership in bringing the global arms trade under control. In particular, it falls to the suppliers to acknowledge a longer-term self-interest in reducing the worst excesses of their sales competition. This means controlling the escalation of technology transfers in weapons production, and addressing the problems of verifying the end-use of dual-use technology transfers. Economic forces and changes in the defence industry have thus far stifled concerns about conventional arms proliferation. This paper argues for regulation of the arms trade through a supply management approach. Rather than concentrating on traditional non-proliferation measures, dominated as they are by sanctions and proscribed items lists, this approach calls for the informal coordination of arms-transfer policies among suppliers. In addition, the inclusion of positive incentives in arms-transfer agreements would give recipients an incentive to 'buy-in' to a system of supply management in conventional arms.

Added to this would be adherence by recipients to supply-side re-transfer restrictions and transparent end-use requirements. By linking positive and negative incentives in this way, the discriminatory aspects of collaboration among suppliers are balanced by ensured access for the recipients to reasonably advanced conventional arms. The participation of second-tier producers in this exercise could be encouraged through relaxing existing export control regimes whichaffect those countries. Again, a 'withholdable' positive incentive for encouraging compliance would alter the increasingly dubious enforcement of expansive restrictions against countries that are essential participants in future multilateral control efforts. The redesign of the Coordinating Committee for Multilateral Export Controls (Cocom) currently in progress provides a valuable opportunity to achieve this essential shift in policy. Beyond the states of the former WTO, other countries should also be integrated into a renewed multilateral control framework. Without their participation, control of conventional arms proliferation will not be possible.

Ad hoc policy coordination in supply management would encourage the growth of constituencies in each of the major suppliers that would support a more disciplined attitude towards arms exports. This approach is not disarmament; rather, it is an exercise in confidence-building and transparency enhancement measures. It is not fully arms control either, because an international consensus against the sale of weapons is absent. Strategies aimed at supply management focus on the stabilisation of global defence markets. Only if this is accomplished will other, more grandiose, calls for conventional arms control have a chance of gaining a fair hearing.

I. SUPPLY-SIDE COMPETITION IN THE GLOBAL ARMS TRADE

The aggressive pursuit of export markets for arms by suppliers is expanding the availability of conventional weapons. Since the end of the Cold War the dominant suppliers of arms have been the Western industrial nations. These countries are also reducing their domestic arms procurement, further increasing the importance of export markets to their defence firms. Western states do not want to control the proliferation of conventional arms. Similarly, suppliers in Russia and China are unwilling to practise unilateral restraint in the face of Western sales in the developing world. Western sales of advanced conventional arms are expanding in relative terms. The spread of advanced weapons is increasing the danger that conflicts will intensify in both lethality and scope. In turn, the weapons sold by advanced states to developing countries may well be used against them, as the 1991 Gulf War illustrated on a limited scale.

The post-Cold War arms trade
The international arms trade is in long-term decline as a result of falling arms procurement in the developing world in the 1980s and the end of the Cold War. Defence budgets the world over are decreasing. This means that defence firms with excess production capacity are now searching for export markets to maintain current levels of employment and technology. Because industrial restructuring cannot take place overnight, this situation is likely to persist for some time. Policymakers thus face some difficult choices. First, they can dismantle current productive capacity, and accept responsibility for the losses in employment and technologies that result. Second, governments can encourage defence firms to seek exports in order to preserve defence industries. The latter option has dominated the international arms market since 1990. In the long term, however, falling world markets make this option unsustainable. In the interim period, export promotion by supplier countries increases the intensity of producer competition in the defence market.

As Table 1 shows, Russia has seen a particularly steep decline in its export share since 1988. Proportionally, its share of new arms-transfer agreements fell from 40% of the world total in 1988 to 6% in 1992. The figures also indicate, however, that the overall global arms trade is in decline. The United States and Western Europe have been more successful at maintaining their export levels, but these too have fallen over the last five years. Russia's drop in export orders is due to the end

Table 1: Arms Transfers to Developing Countries by Supplier, 1988–92 (in millions of constant 1992 dollars)[1]

	1988	1989	1990	1991	1992	Total
US	10,058	8,361	19,485	13,965	13,565	81,628
Russia	14,130	11,676	10,665	5,920	1,300	118,423
France	1,506	4,448	3,232	2,756	3,800	23,057
UK	811	1,112	1,616	2,041	2,400	33,756
China	2,896	1,779	2,262	408	100	17,044
Germany	232	445	323	1,021	700	5,262
Italy	232	222	215	0	400	3,685
All other European	2,201	2,224	2,478	1,531	800	26,743
All others	3,359	1,890	1,939	919	800	16,868
Total	35,423	32,157	42,215	28,562	23,865	326,465

of the Iran–Iraq War in 1987, and to the disintegration of its sales relationships with states in Eastern Europe. More generally, Russia's falling credibility as an international actor has damaged its image as a reliable arms supplier. This has inhibited its defence enterprises from competing effectively in global markets.

Even prior to this situation, however, Russian hard-currency earnings from its defence exports were lower than many Western estimates. Under the old Soviet system, arms were transferred on concessional terms, with payments frequently spread over 20 years with low or negligible interest rates on loans. In addition, counter-trade with countries like China and India meant that the financial returns to Russian arms producers were not reflected in the actual physical volume of defence trade. Licensed production of arms with these two countries also reduced the income from arms exports.[2] More recently, Russia has tried to insist on hard-currency payments for its weapons, but has been forced to abandon this approach because its principal customers were unable to meet these terms.[3]

The recent success of US and Western European efforts at sales promotion is primarily due to the outcome of the 1991 Gulf War. Each of the major Western combatant countries signed long-term supply agreements with Kuwait, Saudi Arabia and the United Arab Emirates (UAE) with a view to building up friendly regional military holdings.[4] Because of the overwhelming dominance of US forces in the conflict, US defence firms received the lion's share of the post-war weapons orders. The distribution of arms sales after the war (in 1992) thus largely reflected the participation of Western states in the Gulf conflict as reflected in Table 2.

Table 2: Regional Arms-Transfer Agreements 1985–92 (in millions of current US dollars)[5]

	Asia		Near East		Latin America		Africa	
	85–88	89–92	85–88	89–92	85–88	89–92	85–88	89–92
US	6,613	15,764	13,547	35,571	1,295	1380	421	139
Russia	23,500	18,000	28,400	6,300	11,400	400	9,800	2,700
France	700	6,500	5,100	6300	1,000	600	600	100
UK	1,100	3,500	20,000	3,000	200	300	0	100
China	1,100	2,100	9,100	1,700	0	0	100	400
Germany	1,500	100	500	1,900	100	300	100	0
Italy	200	100	1,500	400	300	300	200	100
All other European	2,600	1,300	10,900	4,700	1,800	200	700	300
All others	800	1,000	6,400	2,700	1,000	500	1,200	900
Major W. European	3,500	10,200	27,100	11,600	1,600	1500	900	300
Total	38,113	48,364	95,447	62,571	17,095	3,980	13,121	4,739

A regional breakdown of arms sales reveals further the changing market of the principal arms suppliers. It is clear that there is considerable regional variation in sales success. East Asian countries, for example, have increased their arms purchases in recent years. The high economic growth rates of these countries allow them to replace ageing aircraft and naval vessels without straining government budgets.[6] As Table 2 indicates, however, Russia has also been able to maintain its own defence exports to Asia – though in this case sales to China and India dominate the scene – with few exports to East Asia.

Existing political conflicts, such as the dispute between China and Taiwan, and the armed impasse between North and South Korea are two of the leading sources of weapons demand in Asia. Both South

Korea and Taiwan wish to gain domestic technological and economic benefits from their defence acquisitions. Regional defence modernisation programmes allow states to demand significant offset and licensed production benefits in arms-transfer agreements. Competition among suppliers for this business has escalated the diffusion of technology in the defence trade, and promises to increase considerably the defence industrial capabilities of the region's states.[7] The smaller sales volume in Latin America reflects the relatively small number of regional tensions in that area. In Sub-Saharan Africa, acquisitions of major weapons systems are dwarfed by the black market in small arms – the size of which is inherently difficult to estimate.

The Stockholm International Peace Research Institute (SIPRI) offers a slightly different description of the global arms trade. According to its figures, the trade in major weapons systems peaked in 1987, and fell in subsequent years. As Table 3 indicates, the developing world accounted for the majority of defence imports during this period.

Table 3: The Trade in Major Conventional Weapons (in millions of constant 1990 US dollars)[8]

	1983	1984	1985	1986	1987	1988	1989	1990	1991	1992
World Total	45,006	43,098	40,106	42,964	46,555	40,034	38,133	29,972	24,470	18,405
Developing World	30,584	29,345	26,356	28,295	31,775	23,688	21,623	17,682	13,240	9,320
Industrialised World	14,422	13,752	13,750	14,668	14,780	16,346	16,510	12,290	11,230	9,086
Middle East	14,865	14,350	12,350	12,489	16,003	9,901	5,912	6,918	4,714	4,138
ASEAN	1,272	1,352	1,160	1,137	1,398	1,417	955	1,048	1,560	1,060

Table 3 indicates the continuing importance of sales to the Middle East in global defence trade. The decline in real defence imports probably stems from the hard-currency difficulties of a number of Middle Eastern states owing to the fall in world oil prices, and from a slower pace of acquisitions as previously purchased weapons are absorbed into regional arsenals. East Asian countries have increased their imports of conventional wepaons, although the proportion of their

10

GDP devoted to defence spending continues to decline. The high growth rates of these economies mean that they can sustain long-term modernisation programmes. However, under no circumstances should these be interpreted as representing an arms race.[9]

The global arms trade is thus in long-term decline. Policy-makers in the leading supplier countries face the problem of preserving defence industries in a time of shrinking foreign and domestic demand. Exports offer only a short-term solution. Domestic restructuring of defence industries means that governments must choose among defence firms: in effect selecting some companies for survival and others for dissolution and bankruptcy.

Political barriers to supply-side restraint

During the Cold War, international politics determined the character of global arms transfers. In the post-Cold War period, however, domestic economic imperatives have become the dominant factor. Defence exporters faced with declining orders look to foreign markets to maintain production levels, and as a means of financing continuing R&D in weapons and dual-use technologies. Western governments have encouraged this, as it coincides with their diminishing willingness (or ability) to subsidise weapons research and production. In addition, increasing unemployment in defence industries confronts supplier governments with difficult political choices regarding financial support to defence firms. By adopting a market approach, policy-makers thus avoid difficult political decisions regarding industry dismantlement and the displacement of workers.

DOMESTIC POLITICS AND EXPORT RESTRAINT

Because policy-makers focus on their own internal political problems, more diffuse international policy interests – such as conventional weapons proliferation – receive less attention. Supplier governments have thus far been unwilling to agree on a clear definition of weapons exports which can be deemed 'destabilising', or on the naming of 'dangerous' destinations to which conventional arms should not be transferred. This contrasts with the extensive policies of technology denial by the major industrial nations in the nuclear, chemical and biological areas.[10]

The absence of agreement among conventional arms suppliers means that proliferation control policies have yet to take shape. Restraint on exports is subordinated to the economic needs of weapons producers, and to the political needs of supplier governments. Addressing the domestic sources of export incentives means accepting, at least in the short run, that coordinated export restraint is likely to be defeated by strong internal lobbies favouring foreign sales. This is not to say, however, that the international political and economic environment cannot be shaped over the longer term to be more hospitable to proposals for restraint.

Of particular relevance to the new arms market is the break-up of the Soviet Union. Most of its defence industrial capacity is concentrated in Russia and Ukraine.[11] In turn, Russia possesses most of the aerospace, nuclear, chemical and heavy industrial infrastructure of the former Soviet Union. Russia faces a costly and prolonged transition to a market economy. Within that process is an even more complex programme of defence conversion, industry privatisation and dismantlement. Russia has announced that it intends to fund part of this conversion through foreign currency earnings from arms exports.[12]

In spite of their pronounced lack of success in securing export orders, managers of Russian defence enterprises remain convinced of the long-term economic value of their skills and products. The Russian government has approached the US in the hope of negotiating a market share in the arms trade. These approaches were framed within a broader concept of political collaboration between the two countries aimed at improving efforts to resolve international conflicts.[13] Attempts at joint ventures with Western firms have met with little success, partly because such efforts still confront legal barriers on technology transfers to former WTO countries. These joint ventures are, in any case, unlikely to address the widespread over-capacity that afflicts both Western and Russian defence industries. Concerns with technology security and potentially lucrative dual-use technology spin-offs are likely to impede these collaborations for the foreseeable future.[14]

For other states in the former Soviet Union, the possession of large inventories of military equipment presents both a medium-term problem and an economic opportunity. These countries could gain from selling arms at cut prices, and might be able to fund the modernisation of their defence industries – thereby making them more suitable partners for Western firms in the future. It is even possible that the reduced export dependence of these countries may make them *more* attractive as joint venture partners than firms in either Russia or Ukraine. Because these countries (i.e., principally the Baltic states) are unlikely to be competitors with the leading suppliers, constraints on commercial transfers of production technology may be weaker, thus fostering faster globalisation of defence industries.[15]

The production capacity of Ukraine and Russia threatens to upset established patterns of equipment supply due to two factors: price levels; and technology content. Cut-price transfers of advanced combat aircraft and main battle tanks could alter the balance of power in particular regions.[16] In turn, the transfer of production technologies to arms recipients adds to the indigenous productive bases of these countries. China in particular is insisting on the transfer of critical technologies in its agreements to purchase MiG-29s and Su-27s. Over the long term these transfers may be much more important than weapons sales for the global diffusion of defence technologies.

The political difficulties of coordinated supplier restraint reflect the deeper economic conflicts of interest among defence producers. Conventional arms proliferation is simply not a significant concern to policy-makers. The need to maintain defence-sector employment and avoid the loss of critical technological capabilities dominates defence industrial planning. In the case of particularly controversial transfers, *ad hoc* policy responses designed to prevent the transfer of proscribed technologies through third parties are the rule. Re-transfer restrictions, informal diplomatic approaches and background discussions are the dominant forms of official intervention. Each of these approaches is designed to lessen the diplomatic costs of forcing foreign governments publicly to withdraw from a sale, thereby signifying the second-order significance of the arms trade for policy-makers.[17] Over the long term, reductions in the size of defence industries will change (although perhaps not reduce entirely) the political pressure on governments to encourage exports. Until then, unilateral sales restraint will remain a hostage to the perceived good will of trade competitors, and to the weakening consensus on policing the sale of advanced weapons through third parties.[18]

EXPORTS AND DEFENCE SECTOR ADJUSTMENT

A significant part of the management problems experienced by advanced industrial countries as a result of reductions in domestic defence procurement is caused by the restructuring of industries at the prime contractor and subcontractor levels. Considerable national variation is evident in restructuring efforts. In the United States, a number of defence contractors have sold their less profitable businesses in order to concentrate on high profit areas where they are able to dominate markets. General Dynamics (GD), the manufacturer of the F-16 fighter aircraft, is following this strategy, and has sold its aircraft unit to Lockheed. Lockheed has continued production of the F-16 and is seeking foreign and domestic (US) orders extending to the end of the century.[19]

GD also sold its space-launch vehicle (SLV) unit to Martin-Marietta, in a controversial transaction involving the return to Marietta, in cash, of projected budget savings by the US government.[20] In turn, the company is concentrating its activities in the defence sector, attempting to purchase smaller companies with significant order backlogs. GD, however, is seeking to increase the returns to shareholders in the short run by distributing proceeds from the sale of businesses through special dividend payments. GD's share price has also risen during its divestment programme, although it seems inevitable that the pace of its sales must fall off – as the number (and value) of its remaining businesses is reduced. Martin-Marietta's efforts illustrate the other dominant strategy: a reconcentration in defence activities, with selective diversification into dual-use areas.

Subcontractor industrial adjustment illustrates a different pattern. In the United States the number of subcontractors has been shrinking for the best part of a decade.[21] This has been caused by certain contractors seeking to force cost reductions from their principal suppliers. In addition, the adoption of 'Total Quality Management' and 'Just In Time' inventory controls has altered the relationship of prime contractors to subcontractors. These innovations emphasise statistical control techniques in production management and design. Subcontractors must now meet increasingly stringent quality and inventory response criteria in order to maintain their ties with traditional customers. Increasingly cut-throat competition among subcontractors has resulted in some firms losing their traditional customers, leading to either diversification from the defence industry or bankruptcy.[22]

A second cause of shrinkage in the subcontractor tier is the financial squeeze. Diminishing subsidies and a harsh acquisitions environment mean that smaller companies are less able to gain access to the capital necessary to stay at the cutting edge of technology.[23] The result is the continued closure of smaller defence firms, either because of acquisition by larger enterprises, or because they are no longer able to maintain a financially viable scale of production.

Defence firms in Western Europe have adapted in different ways to companies in North America. Firms in Europe tend to be smaller than in the US because they serve smaller markets. In turn, these firms have generally been less innovative in weapons technology. National defence firms in Europe have begun to create transnational joint ventures in order to serve the Western European part of the North Atlantic Treaty Organisation (NATO) through common programmes and technology sharing. Examples of these ventures include projects under EUCLID (a European technology development programme created in the aftermath of the US Strategic Defense Initiative), the Eurocopter consortium, Eurodynamics, and the Eurofighter 2000 consortium.[24] State ownership also plays a much greater role in the management of the defence sector in Europe than in the United States. At the same time, there is variation within Europe, with the United Kingdom possessing a mostly private defence sector, whereas France's defence industries are almost all within the public sector.[25] Government-owned companies appear less able than their private-sector counterparts to change strategy rapidly in uncertain market conditions. The political difficulty of closing defence factories and reducing R&D funding leads governments to spread hard decisions over a number of years, or to seek to avoid them entirely through privatisation schemes aimed at shifting the responsibility for employment reductions on to market forces.[26]

Because of its higher level of state ownership, it is likely that industrial restructuring will happen more slowly in Western Europe than in the United States. With important exceptions, the political costs of high unemployment in the defence sector remain an unpalatable alternative to continued subsidies. In the short run, then, the dominant strategy – as noted above – is to expand export markets in order to retain the basic structure of domestic defence industries. For the reasons discussed above, however, it is not feasible for all suppliers to succeed at this strategy, hence the potential for deadlock among supplier countries.

Proposals for a free-trade zone in defence products arose in the 1980s, and were championed by the then US Ambassador to NATO, William H. Taft IV. Little of substance emerged from these initiatives, however, and European states have instead begun to organise regional collaboration in defence procurement and R&D. Initially, these efforts were launched within the Inter-European Programme Group (IEPG). More recently, the IEPG has been integrated into the Western European Union (WEU) and become known as the Western European Armaments Group (WEAG).[27] This group attempts to foster transparency and a reduction in defence trade barriers among the members of the WEU. While little substantive progress has been achieved, it appears that this regional – rather than Atlanticist – approach to defence trade management will be the focus of future efforts.

The continuing insistence on national defence industrial planning means that the overcapacity of European defence industries is unlikely to be reduced in the near future. In turn, joint ventures created in response to shrinking domestic markets and concerns for market entry are likely to develop slowly. Export promotion is likely to continue, alongside a lengthy debate on the political and economic costs of industrial restructuring in the defence area. National responses, like national defence policies, will differ across the NATO alliance. Private defence firms, more able than government-owned enterprises to adapt to a rapidly changing defence market-place, are more likely to survive the current transition period.

THE ECONOMICS OF DUAL-USE TRADE
The economic factors that discourage arms sellers from unilateral restraint are significantly stronger in dual-use technologies. The advanced industrial nations are all adopting policies designed to encourage the development of high-technology industries. The products of these industries are designed for civil markets, but have inherently dual or multiple uses. Industries such as aerospace, jet engine manufacture, semiconductor manufacturing, computer manufacturing, electronics, specialty materials, pharmaceuticals and genetic engineering all involve significant government R&D subsidies. The international trade in these industries significantly exceeds the size of the international arms trade. In manufacturing, defence production made up only 4.9% of US industrial output in 1992.[28] In turn, defence manufacturing itself takes place in a combination of government-owned, contractor operated (GOCO) plants, and private-sector firms which maintain separate commercial and defence sector operations.[29]

Patterns of defence industry–commercial industry interpenetration differ among the major arms suppliers. In the former Soviet Union, for example, no separate civilian goods industry exists. Instead, the defence industrial complex produces goods for both civil and defence purposes, with predictably negative results for the quality of commercial products.[30] In the West, the situation is fundamentally different, with large commercial firms existing side by side with others which sell into both defence and commercial markets. Firms that are involved in both sectors usually operate separate production, accounting and R&D facilities for each sector. Differences in technical specifications in commercial and defence products further separate the two sectors. Lastly, differences in business culture impede the transfer of technical and marketing expertise across the civil/defence sector boundary.[31] Levels of state ownership in these industries reflect the pattern noted above for arms producers. As in defence production, the pace and nature of sectoral adjustment varies in direct relation to the responsiveness of producers to market forces.

In dual-use technologies, commercial firms have a significant advantage over those more closely under state control. More importantly,

16

there is little to prevent commercial firms from entering into joint ventures where compatible business or technological capabilities make mutual gain possible. For state-owned (or closely regulated) firms, concerns about technology security may impede the rapid exploitation of the commercial application of dual-use technologies. Further, the potential for transnational collaboration in dual-use areas confronts the full range of national-security export controls. Indeed, joint ventures may be impossible where state policies interfere with equity markets and deny ownership and control to foreign investors in a critical industry.[32]

NEW EXPORTERS
In the last two decades, countries that were formerly only recipients of arms transfers entered the global market as exporters. These countries, for example Israel, South Africa, South Korea, Brazil, Argentina and North Korea, all managed to export 'knock offs' of more advanced weapons systems for a fraction of the price sought by the established suppliers.[33] Offsets and counter-trade benefits in arms transfers further expand the productive base of these second-tier defence industries, as is discussed in the next section. Offsets and joint production arrangements allow recipients access to technological and economic frameworks linked to an increasingly globalised defence sector. Suppliers encourage this process through the transfer of specially adapted production systems which 'black box' the most critical aspects of complex weapons systems. More than simple weapons assembly, such production activities embody contemporary notions of lean production and just-in-time inventory control.[34] The success of Iraq in building its defence industries during and after the Iran–Iraq War is a sobering reminder that developing states are increasingly capable of achieving technological breakthroughs by exploiting uncontrolled 'third country' suppliers of advanced technology. Access to controlled technologies was also facilitated by Western policies that favoured Iraq when an Iranian victory appeared possible.[35]

The manipulation of arms-supply relationships in foreign policy is a risky business. When nations are at war, they seek to minimise their dependence on any single supplier, and exploit whatever covert means are available to circumvent an embargo. Transfers of arms also take place over an extended period. Today's ally can become tomorrow's adversary. The potential thus exists for major suppliers to face their own weapons in combat, something France experienced in the Gulf War. More generally, suppliers are responsible for spreading arms-production capabilities to an increasing number of developing countries. These transfers mean that future attempts to impose arms embargoes to constrain conflict escalation will be more difficult to achieve, as the number of uncontrolled sources for arms increases (see Table 4).

Table 4: Value of Exports of Major Conventional Weapons by Developing Countries 1983–92 (in constant 1990 dollars)[36]

	1983	1984	1985	1986	1987	1988	1989	1990	1991	1992
Developing World	3,913	3,462	2,565	2,657	4,846	3,688	1,921	1,719	2,163	2,031
LDCs	–	27	–	34	99	3	–	–	2	–

Other issues also inhibit policy coordination among suppliers. The technological sophistication of transferred weapons is increasing as suppliers compete for market share. Russia has transferred Su-27 and MiG-29 aircraft on concessional terms in order to secure foreign buyers. This does not augur well for future technology restrictions. Competition in particular weapons categories is standardising performance in areas such as air-to-air missiles, advanced combat aircraft, surface-to-air (and anti-ballistic) missiles and land combat vehicles.[37] Similarities of weapons design and technical specifications have other effects beyond the scope of this paper, but note can be taken that the politics of coalition warfare (e.g., the Gulf War) mandate that countries achieve the maximum degree of equipment interoperability prior to a conflict. World products establish a common technical basis for this sort of collaboration, and also transform the logistics of combined operations in the event of hostilities.[38] As such, this technical trend is complementary to a political goal of ensuring that armed forces of the developing world (e.g., those of the Persian Gulf States) are integrated with those of their principal arms suppliers, the oil-dependent countries of Western Europe and North America.

DIRECT AND INDIRECT OFFSET BENEFITS
Offset benefits are important because they highlight two areas: first, the importance of direct technical support to fielded weapons systems in developing states; and second, the 'catalytic' character of infrastructure investments in developing economies. Direct assistance in operating imported weapons is provided by the supplier. Developing states are starting to demand a high level of local participation in this aspect

of the arms trade. For example, Turkey has achieved considerable progress in technology acquisition through the MIKES joint venture created with US Contractor Loral to manufacture parts of the Rapport III integrated electronic warfare (EW) system for its F-16 aircraft. Thomson-CSF of France has established Thomson-Tefken Radar and Thomson-Tefken Technoloji in partnership with the Turkish firm Tefken Holdings to build 10 of 14 Thomson TRS 22XX mobile air-surveillance radars. In each transaction the Turkish government demanded, and received, technology transfers designed to establish 'the seeds for new projects for the advanced products that our country needs'.[39] Beyond the warehousing of spare parts, recipients now insist upon the creation of joint venture companies to provide continuous support to their forces in the field.[40]

Infrastructure investments are important because they increase the productivity of local workers. Supplier countries who have pledged an agreed level of offset benefits rely upon local skills and institutions to reduce the costs of their commitments. If sales and manufacturing personnel of the recipient countries are inadequately trained, this can inhibit the delivery of prompt offset benefits of special importance in highly competitive arms-transfer agreements. For example, offset agreements signed by Saudi Arabia and other Gulf States have faced problems meeting domestic employment projections because of a lack of indigenous skilled workers. Foreign workers have allowed these deals to continue, but at the price of a smaller contribution by the local workforce.[41] Paradoxically then, offset obligations mean that developed states benefit from raising the technological level of local workers. A more adaptable and well-educated workforce in the recipient country will be able to absorb more rapidly the skills necessary to make a joint venture or offset company financially viable. In turn, the global nature of the arms trade allows recipients to participate in the international economy in high value-added areas otherwise beyond their capabilities.[42] Another example of this situation is the construction of an aircraft overhaul facility in the UAE by Boeing. Regional air transport needs aside, this centre owes its location to an offset agreement involving Boeing and other Western defence contractors.

It is easy to envisage collaboration between 'friendly' countries and leading arms suppliers to limit the re-transfer of exported products. A long-term political and economic relationship forms an effective basis for such cooperation. Other countries, however, are likely to do everything in their power to circumvent multilateral restrictions. This is especially true of so-called 'pariah' or rogue nations such as North Korea, who see their exports as a symbol of independence from great-power intimidation, and as an important source of foreign exchange. Beyond punitive measures to prevent such countries from violating internationally agreed arms-transfer limits, it is difficult to see what new approaches would encourage their compliance.

If the problem of rogue states were not enough, it is often difficult to differentiate a weapons-production and industrialisation strategy from a more benign indigenisation of dual-use technologies. As is true for developed countries, developing states see access to dual-use technologies as fundamental to their economic development. Defence industries can make contributions to industrial development, even if they do not provide the most efficient means of attaining developmental goals. Offset benefits in arms transfers can give developing states access to valuable technologies on concessional terms. As such, they can subsidise industrialisation and increase local skills applicable to international trade.

Technology acquisition strategies are frequently aimed at the creation of domestic substitutes for imported items. In turn, it is hoped that these products can then be improved and exported as a means of financing further industrial growth. Countries as varied as Brazil, Malaysia, Singapore and Indonesia have all adopted Import-Substituting-Industrialisation (ISI) strategies at one time or another since the Second World War. Their examples point to a problem created by existing approaches to supply-side restraint which are aimed at preventing the spread of developmentally useful technologies. Technology restrictions aimed at second-tier countries – those which have achieved some degree of export-quality technological capacity – are perceived to inflict serious economic costs on their targets. At the same time, these new arms producers are the very countries that are increasingly essential to supply-side discussions on arms-transfer regulation. Clearly, a different strategy is in order if integration of these new technology centres into multilateral technology control regimes is to be achieved.

In search of supplier self-restraint
It is clear from the economic and political factors affecting suppliers that the short-term prospects for negotiated restraint are extremely poor. All that has been agreed is a transparency enhancement measure – the United Nations Arms Transfer Register.[43] The Register itself is a promising, though limited, proposal. It sets up a system of reporting, whereby participating states provide information regarding their imports and exports of weapons and military equipment in seven categories.[44] The first year of the UN Register revealed more information

than many critics had expected. In turn, the level of participation was also encouraging, with 83 states providing some form of information.[45] Nevertheless, it is clear that a shift from notification of arms transfers after the event to prior notification of *agreements* is not presently under consideration.

Political and economic differences among suppliers place clear limits on the 'deepening' of the Register. Controversies which may result from recipients not wishing to release information about their weapons purchases may also limit supplier incentives to participate. Similarly, issues of intellectual property and proprietary information must be addressed if the Register is to progress beyond a simple report of annual deliveries of weapons. The question arises of what political value the Register will be if it does not improve the potential for movement towards some sort of arms-transfer regulation. This implies that the Register is hostage to the willingness of states to move beyond a benign confidence-building measure towards more meaningful information sharing and political bargaining. It is likely that any improvements in the provision of information will be tied to specific instances of regional conflict resolution and war termination.[46] It is only under these conditions that the major arms suppliers seem able to overcome their export incentives.

The challenge of supply-side controls lies in the conflicting economic and political interests of the major suppliers. Added to this is the increasingly fragmented nature of supply networks.[47] This fact, itself the result of the spread of arms industries worldwide, is reinforced by the market power of recipients and the increasing importance of offset benefits and licensed production in arms-transfer agreements. These trends also have implications for the regulation of global technology diffusion, an issue addressed in the next chapter. Joint ventures among defence firms in the supplier states provide new avenues for inadvertent technology transfers. Where new subsidiaries in recipient countries are created through lucrative offset agreements, proliferation of advanced technologies becomes a significant new danger. The international trade in arms will become much less transparent, and thus less easy to regulate. The UN Register, for this reason, needs to be expanded to include production for domestic use – or domestic holdings – in order to capture this increasingly important aspect of defence production.[48]

More generally, the convergence of supply-side economic and political forces against unilateral restraint mandates a collective search for another option. That option involves a coordinated response to *shared* political and economic dilemmas which lead to a bias in the global arms transfer system against a reduction in export volume. In fact, the needs of defence producers for foreign markets are likely to change over time in response to the post-Cold War restructuring. In the West, this process could produce smaller, more concentrated defence industries, which will be more appropriately sized for their domestic markets, and – with luck – much less export-oriented. Rationalisation of defence industries through mergers and acquisitions (more prevalent in the United States) and transnational joint ventures (more the model in Western Europe) means that over the medium to long term the export orientations of these industries will undergo a profound change. This has implications for the willingness of governments to share political costs and commercial risks in refraining from sales to potentially lucrative markets – where they exist.[49]

In the former Soviet Union, and among the new class of second-tier exporters, a parallel process of adjustment may have contrary consequences for the regulation of arms transfers. In the former Soviet Union, industries are facing drastic downsizing, together with attempts to create new international linkages as the basis for new arms-supply networks. The presence of Russian arms manufacturers at the world's many arms expositions testifies to their interest in generating new foreign business. Potentially unanswerable, however, is the effect of changes in Russian *domestic* procurement that will undoubtedly be the determining factor in the restructuring of its defence industrial complex. On the premise that domestic orders will still overshadow any likely foreign sales, it remains to be seen whether the export orientation of Russian defence producers will shift in the same direction as their Western counterparts.

Producers in the second tier, such as Israel, Brazil and South Africa, face a potentially harsh international market, and a return to their smaller market niches after the temporary expansion of their sales during the Iran–Iraq War.[50] These industries promise, however, to remain active in the upgrade and spares markets, which, according to some estimates, dwarf the future demand for whole weapons systems.[51] International regulation of arms flows relies upon the participation of all aspects of defence production and weapons system innovation. The second-tier are unlikely to restrain themselves when their larger competitors are entering previously closed markets. More generally, the dual civil–military industrial strategies of a number of these countries mean that any punitive actions are likely to result in non-compliance with international proliferation control regimes.[52] Economic growth remains uppermost in the minds of policy-makers in developing countries – alongside concerns about national sovereignty. The continued application of export controls to these countries is both counter-productive and likely to hinder efforts at integrating them into new supplier groupings. The next chapter discusses the structure of the principal supplier groups, and focuses on the challenges facing traditional export controls.

II. SUPPLIER ORGANISATIONS AND REGULATORY APPROACHES

Suppliers have organised exclusive groups for the management of technology transfers. These institutions share common characteristics, most importantly their exclusivity of membership, and the application of discriminatory controls against non-members. Examples of supplier organisations operating on the periphery of the international arms trade are: the Missile Technology Control Regime (MTCR); the (London) Nuclear Suppliers' Group (NSG); the Australia (Chemical Suppliers') Group; the US–Japan Supercomputer regime; and the former Cocom (see Appendix for a more detailed description of these regimes). These institutions are designed to restrict the spread of technologies associated with weapons of mass destruction.

The increasing number of dual-use technologies covered by these regimes means that they provide an important restriction on international trade. These groups all have a similar approach to the regulation of technology transfers. First, they have overlapping memberships, with the exception of Cocom, whose successor will likely include states from the former Soviet Union and Eastern Europe.[1] The core group members are the NATO countries, with neutral states such as Austria, Switzerland and Finland enjoying special relations with control regimes. Basically, these ties ensure that so-called 'third country sources' do not circumvent broader multilateral controls.[2] More recently, the states of the former Warsaw Pact have been included in discussions on reforming export controls. These moves have thus far met with only limited success, but over the longer term the involvement of these countries is essential.[3]

Common regime characteristics
In addition to their overlapping membership, supplier groups also share a basic approach to regulating technology trade. Based on technology denial, these groups aim to prevent the creation of trade channels outside of established – and well-policed – supply networks.[4] This approach has four elements. First, supplier groups maintain lists of proscribed items requiring special licensing procedures when transferred to non-members. These restrictions operate whether a transfer takes place through a discrete product, or within an industrial process.

Second, there are lists of restricted destinations, even if a formal blacklist is absent. Most typically, recipients receive security classifications that allow them to import items up to a defined level, after which a formal appeal process governs whether an export restriction will be waived. Such waivers flow from diplomatic considerations, or from a state joining a supplier organisation.[5]

Third, an international protocol or items list exists to mediate differences in members' national export controls which create the potential for the non-uniform application of technology restrictions. Lists such as the Cocom International Industrial List (comprised of dual-use technologies), the International Munitions List, and the International Atomic Energy Control List coordinate technical restrictions in member-countries and focus discussions on policing illicit applications and regime circumvention. More generally, these lists provide focal points for bargaining between states on supplier restrictions. In this way they form the backbone of supplier restrictions.

Last, supplier groups allow member-states to share intelligence information on the behaviour of potential proliferator nations. This allows for a more focused attack on particular countries, and for continuous assessments of target nations in terms of their established supplier–recipient relations and access to advanced technologies. Information on the diffusion of applications thus fosters the removal of items from controlled lists that are either obsolete, or available from several uncontrolled sources.[6] Information sharing also promotes the policing of a trade increasingly dominated by large multinational corporations with operations in both the developed and developing worlds. The diffusion of technology caused by intra-firm transactions across national boundaries is a particularly significant problem.[7]

Problems of technology denial
The end of the Cold War undermined the Western consensus on supplier technology controls, in particular that on proscribed technologies and restricted destinations. With the collapse of the Soviet Union and the WTO, the argument for broad restrictions on technology access and transfer is simply less compelling. The significance of this is illustrated by the rapid removal of controls on those countries within the Cocom framework.[8] More recently, Cocom itself is being disbanded, as it is widely held to have achieved its goal – and, therefore, to have outlived its usefulness. The pace of trade competition among allied nations makes unilateral restrictions on technology trade increasingly untenable.[9] This is particularly important with regard to the United States, whose more restrictive controls have historically formed the backbone of multilateral restrictions.[10]

The prospect for more focused international restrictions on technology flows is also lessened by the increasing number of unrestricted sources of dual-use technologies. Countries such as Brazil, Argentina, India and Pakistan are now beginning to enter the supply-side of the market for sensitive technologies. These countries' emerging ballistic-missile, nuclear and chemical–industrial complexes mean that international controls are providing increasingly ineffective barriers to technology diffusion. More importantly, firms in developed countries often have lucrative commercial relationships with developing-world research and industrial concerns. This in turn creates economic incentives that promote the transnational dispersal of production and R&D activities, further reducing the feasibility of strategic embargoes.[11]

The increasingly transnational nature of key dual-use industries is creating new supply networks for technology trade. The spread of strategic alliances and joint ventures between firms in different countries also provides a daunting challenge for transfer restrictions. Definitions of technology transfer, broader concerns over intellectual property, and the links between public- and private-sector research, all affect the viability of export controls. Also important in this area are the dual-sector (civil and military) industrial strategies followed by many developing countries.[12] State involvement in establishing local technical and manufacturing industries in the developing world means that it is harder to separate public policy from commercial and proliferation-related concerns. Joint ventures created by offset and licensed production arrangements are particularly likely to challenge established rules governing technology transfer.[13] Discriminatory treatment of recipients aggravates political relations between North and South at a time when closer political contacts might help curb proliferation. Policy-makers thus face a dilemma regarding the exact point at which continuing technology restrictions on particular countries cease to contribute to proliferation control, and instead place at risk broader concerns about stability and world order.[14]

Technology denial is also a victim of its own success. The end of the Cold War has produced calls to expand the membership of supplier groups to include the states of the former Soviet Union. Almost without exception, these countries lack anything approaching a Western-style export control system. While some progress in this direction has occurred in Eastern Europe (most notably in Hungary), the dropping of technology transfer restrictions with the former Soviet Union would considerably weaken Western export controls. The porous nature of the Commonwealth of Independent States (CIS) borders offers a tempting opportunity for countries interested in acquiring restricted technologies.[15] Western nations must balance the economic costs of continued controls against the political problems which have been created by targeting the new democracies of Eurasia as restricted destinations. The creation of working export control systems within the CIS is the best way to ensure the integrity of *Western* technology controls as supplier groups expand their membership.

The number and kind of export restrictions further complicate the administration of multilateral rules. The large number and variety of items in the dual-use technology category mean that many commercial products fall within restrictive areas. Trade competition (e.g., in semiconductor manufacturing equipment, applications of x-ray lithography, supercomputers) means that governments are loathe to restrict exports without guarantees from partners that they will do the same. As in the international arms trade, states are under pressure to expand the market share of their national firms, while at the same time seeking to protect domestic firms from the exclusionary practices of other governments. The situation is thus one of deadlock, where technology producers seek to protect themselves from the high costs of exclusion from increasingly closed markets. In political terms, this means that agreements on transfer restrictions are hostage to the conflicts of economic interest. Economic competition overwhelms supplier self-restraint so frequently that the feasibility of institutionalised limits is very low.[16]

The rapid progress in technological R&D presents a further barrier to tight regulatory oversight. The numerous technical applications stemming from applied research makes it difficult to predict the exact patterns of illicit usage that presage proliferation. This was illustrated by the three unknown projects for the enrichment of uranium and the separation of plutonium which were discovered in Iraq by the International Atomic Energy Agency (IAEA) following the 1991 Gulf War.[17]

The growth of R&D in developing countries means that they are increasingly able to produce less sophisticated versions of first-tier weapons systems and munitions. Care must be taken that regulation does not trigger a decision by a recipient state to develop an indigenous capability wholly outside international surveillance. The examples of South Africa in arms manufacturing, and India in nuclear and ballistic-missile technologies show the unpredictable effects of international embargoes.[18]

The Cold War clarified issues in technology transfer restrictions to an extent that will not be repeated under post-Cold War conditions. Export controls aimed at the Soviet Union were critically dependent on US superiority in weapons and dual-use technologies. Even here, however, recent years have produced an erosion in US technological dominance of its allies in Western Europe and Japan. Additionally, the US frequently adopted unilateral restraints on trade, but the economic costs of this position are now viewed as untenable by US political élites. As a consequence, the US now favours much more selectivity, and is unlikely to allow its export controls to be more restrictive than those of its allies. In any case, no clear Western consensus now exists on a post-Cold War export controls strategy. While proliferation control may provide a general framework for *ad hoc* coordination, it is unlikely to foster the level of institutionalised consultation evident during the Cold War.

Strategic embargoes and commercial trade
Cold War export controls implemented a strategic embargo against the Soviet Union and its allies. All supplier groups, to varying degrees, reflect this heritage in their modes of operation and membership. Especially important in groups such as Cocom and the MTCR were political differences between the United States and its key allies. As discussed above, the divergence of allied economic interests has led to the US definition of restricted technologies being contested. This situation has also created disputes over which countries should be denied access to dual-use technologies. Both these issues – economic competition and disagreements over potential proliferators – reflect a more profound crisis concerning US leadership of the Western community. If the US can no longer supply the 'hard core' of proliferation control in supplier groups, how is a strong consensus to be sustained ?

The decline of US leadership
Although the United States remains the world's only superpower, its economic dependence on international trade is now higher than ever. As a trading nation, the US is able to use its still considerable influence to open foreign markets perceived as closed to its business firms. During the Cold War, shared threat perceptions reconciled market opening with a defence of the 'free world'. US alliance leadership thus translated into defence of an economic area, in addition to the more mundane concern with military security. With the demise of the threat from the East, economic policies partly influenced by the vision of a free trade area under siege are being abandoned.

Western European states are now the leading competitors of the United States in global technology markets, with the notable addition of Japan. As US concerns with economic competitiveness grow, technology issues – and restrictive trading practices – become the subject of multilateral discussions. Economic competitiveness thus adds to existing irritants in political relations among the Western allies. Bargaining inside established technology control regimes is likely to become more complicated as a result. US leadership of existing multilateral regimes increases the potential for these developments to create a wholesale crisis of legitimacy in Western control efforts.

US technological leadership has also been affected by the changing importance of defence technology investments to economic competitiveness. During the Cold War, US defence research was said to provide 'spin-off' benefits to civilian industries.[19] This belief was particularly strong in the aerospace, automotive and electronic industries, where US firms set world standards in technology and customer responsiveness. More recently, however, arguments regarding spin-off benefits have been criticised as failing to take into account the negative impact of defence spending on the selection of investment priorities in the macroeconomy.[20]

The technical and performance specifications of military systems frequently bear little or no relation to mainstream commercial applications.[21] In designing commercial products, a rapid response to changing market conditions is required. In addition, the multinational nature of companies forces them to undertake market research when adapting their products to different locales. In weapons design, however, specific requirements are generated in response to technical criteria determined partially by defence firms themselves. This competitive environment is unlikely to deliver low-cost weapons systems able to meet the varying needs of different countries. While the rate of technical innovation in military systems continues to accelerate, the costs of the completed systems frequently allow only small-scale procurement of weapons. This means that exports are necessary to lower the unit cost of arms for domestic acquisition, further increasing the incentives for foreign sale.

The relative economic weakness of the US became manifest during the rise of Western European and Japanese industrial competitors in the 1960s and 1970s. In industries as varied as telecommunications, computers and precision machine tools, Japan and Western Europe (most importantly, Germany) were able to match or exceed the sophistication of equipment produced in the United States. In semiconductor manufacturing and electronics, countries such as Singapore, Taiwan, South Korea, Malaysia and Indonesia have all achieved considerable success in producing for world markets. These new industries were created during the period of declining US competitiveness in these very areas. Indeed, US industry became almost wholly concentrated in the defence sector. In Western Europe, industries were frequently protected by their governments as part of national industrial policies.

These producers were given preference in domestic economies, thus preventing US firms from dominating areas designated as essential to sovereignty – such as arms production, telecommunications and computers. The US, however, remained important as a source of weapons technology, as the barriers to entry into many systems areas left Europeans with little option but to seek joint production arrangements with large US firms.[22] Over time, however, this situation changed as Western European defence–industrial consortia formed, frequently with the encouragement of supportive governments. Examples of these consortia include Eurocopter, Euromissile and, in the civil sector, Airbus.[23]

Industrial combinations in Europe involved both commercial- and defence-sector operations. Defence firms were thus forced to be innovative in commercial markets, while at the same time meeting the defence equipment needs of governments. Institutional factors in Europe removed the necessity for clearly separating defence and commercial operations. Governments view these firms as national assets. Correspondingly, these companies are often protected from anti-trust rules.[24] This allowed for technological 'borrowing' between the defence and commercial sectors, which enhanced the performance of both.[25] This subsidisation of industrial production was thus a difficult target for US market-opening policies.[26] Because of the small size of Western European defence markets, firms developed a pattern of joint venture creation as a response to the strength of their larger US competitors. These two factors – mixed (commercial and defence) industrial strategies implemented through national champions, and differences in industry structure because of the greater prevalence of joint ventures – created a pronounced export orientation in European industries.[27]

The post-Cold War setting is thus characterised by industries which demand access to export markets while at the same time having market structures designed for a less competitive global market-place. In turn, US firms that enjoy advantages of size and technological competence are now vulnerable to foreign competitors which have always maintained a presence in commercial markets. This concern complicates negotiations between the US and its closest allies, whom the US accuses of plotting to enter industries still under its dominance. The FSX controversy, in which Japan sought a successor to its inventory of F-16 aircraft, provides a telling example. For a variety of reasons, Japan decided to build a new aircraft on its own. Subsequently, however, American pressure led to the formation of the FSX project with US involvement.[28] Spin-on benefits from commercial-sector activities may have been absorbed more readily by corporations which were not forced to segregate defence and commercial operations. More accurately, however, commercial firms with few defence involvements (e.g., those in Japan and East Asia), have succeeded in increasing the rate at which advanced technology is integrated into new products. Thus the most advanced electronic systems are increasingly embedded in commercial products, not in weapons systems. Indeed, the lengthy product cycles characteristic of advanced weapons contrast increasingly with the rapid turnover of technical generations in commercial areas.[29] Weapons systems increasingly borrow from commercial applications, rather than vice versa. As a consequence, the lack of a viable civil-sector technology base (a relative phenomenon) can have serious consequences for defence industries. In short, the inability to borrow across the commercial–defence-sector boundary can reduce the rate of weapons innovation, and lower the market share of export-oriented industries.

The Clinton Administration is currently in the middle of an extensive revision of the legislation governing national security export controls. Established in the Export Administration Act (EAA), these rules regulate the trade in US-origin technologies which have dual-use or principally weapons applications. This legislation received a one-year extension in 1993, with a view to concluding a revision of the law by 1 June 1994. That target date was missed due to domestic political controversies over the selective relaxation of controls, and the reform of regulations which impose high compliance costs on businesses.[30] There is an increasing level of disagreement regarding the objectives and appropriate measures of export controls administration. Early on in the Clinton Administration there was a split between the incoming officials who favoured a selective relaxation of controls on items that were widely available from third parties, and members of the bureaucracy who favoured the retention of established rules. In turn, the bureaucracy also wished to continue to impose re-export controls on an *ad hoc* basis, something businesses have protested about for a considerable time.[31]

A number of other differences existed between the Clinton Administration's early policy preferences and those of the bureaucracy. Included in these differences were: disagreements over rights of judicial appeal on export control decisions; the imposition of a fixed time period for the processing of export requests; the streamlining of the decision-making process for export requests; and sanctions on firms which violated export regulations. Each of these issues has further delayed the achievement of a consensus on export controls. Congressional dissatisfaction with the Administration's proposals led to the rejection of the first plan for the EAA revision.[32] A different approach sponsored by Sam Gedjenson, Chairman of the House of Foreign Affairs Subcommittee, and supported by business interests now forms the basis for discussion. This plan retains the current use of re-transfer controls on items, including US-origin technologies. This is almost guaranteed to exacerbate trade policy friction with the European allies. At the same time, the legislation would establish limited judicial review of Administration export control decisions, and would set a 30-day processing period for licensing decisions, and a 15-day period for interagency referrals. It remains to be seen when this legislation will be ready for implementation.[33]

Fragmentation of supplier networks

Two groups of countries are changing the nature of the supply-side in arms transfers by creating new channels for weapons transfers to developing states. These countries include former recipients of Western arms (e.g., South Korea, India, Pakistan, Argentina), and a more unpredictable group, the states of the CIS and East-Central Europe. However, the technological state-of-the-art continues to be set by the market leaders in Western Europe and the United States. The expansion and contraction of market niches is critical to the economic viability of these groups of suppliers. For their own part, they seek to position themselves as alternative suppliers of middle-range systems, frequently 'knock-offs' of prior-generation Western (and Soviet) products. The new supply channels transfer both new production and older inventories of surplus arms.

As indicated in Chapter I, the arms trade has declined in size over the last two to three years. Parallel with this was a steeper decline in second-tier arms transfers, mostly due to the conclusion of the Iran–Iraq War, which had given countries like Brazil unprecedented sales success in the Gulf region.[34] China, Israel and North Korea also made significant sales to the states involved in the conflict. The return of the larger Western arms exporters to the region in the 1990s, however, drastically reduced the sales of second-tier countries. Brazil, in particular, was forced to abandon its attempt to sell the *Osorio* main battle tank to Saudi Arabia, as the Saudis bought the US M-1 *Abrams* tank instead.[35] In spite of these reversals, recipient arms acquisition strategies favour the continued presence of these alternate sources of arms and dual-use technologies. Even in the aftermath of the Gulf War, it was evident that regional states wanted to diversify their sources of supply among the major arms-producing participants in the coalition. Niche suppliers were largely shut out of these lucrative contracts, but

32

have every opportunity to re-enter the trade as the market for upgrades and incremental weapons system improvements continues to mature. In addition, Kuwait has decided to diversify its arms suppliers to include Russia and China in order to cement political relations with members of the UN Permanent Five. This diversification strategy is symbolic of the measures used by arms recipients to ensure reliability of supply, while at the same time establishing political contacts with extra-regional states.[36]

The diversification strategies of arms-transfer recipients highlight the availability of significant offsets in defence trade (as discussed in Chapter I), and the increasing integration of defence industries into complex transnational supply networks. Recipient states seek to achieve a number of different goals in purchasing from a variety of different powers:

> Reverse the direction of dependence within particular offset arrangements;
> Create a minimal level of infrastructure in the home country, so as to increase the capacity of local producers to absorb transferred technologies;
> Include the recipient in the transnational production system of the principal arms supplier.

These complementary goals structure the bargaining in arms-transfer agreements, and open the global defence sector to increasing participation by small producers who can meet the changing needs of arms recipients.

The former Soviet Union and technology diffusion
The former Soviet Union (principally Russia) is a critical source of uncertainty in the new landscape of the international arms market. Possessing first-tier weapons technology, Russia and, to a lesser extent, the other successor states, are now entering the arms trade as serious commercial competitors. It is not difficult to imagine the potentially serious consequences if Russia should 'dump' those highly sophisticated arms on the market which represent its best chance of capturing market share. Added to this is the continuing absence of a legislative basis for national export controls in most members of the CIS. Even in Russia, national controls are implemented on the basis of a presidential decree, and not on parliamentary legislation.[37] More importantly, the lack of rigorous border controls in much of the CIS means that Russian controls offer the best chance for stemming the illicit diffusion of dual-use technologies from the former Soviet Union.

Thus, unauthorised technology transfers coi in the law are similarly reinforced by accusations of Western hypocrisy. If Russia adopts arms-export behaviour similar to that of Western nations, significant problems will ensue.

Initially, the use of the arms transfers by Western states to cement their military–technological advantages *vis-à-vis* recipients would become much more difficult in an unrestricted arms-export environment. It is not, however, unambiguously in Russia's interest to press its advantages against Western suppliers. Russia desires collaboration with the West in a number of different areas, including that of converting defence manufacturing capabilities to dual-use or civilian manufacturing. This fact alone should inject a degree of caution into Russian export policies. Russia's renegotiation of its agreement with India to sell cryogenic engines (Glavkosmos and the Indian Space Research Organisation) suggests that these considerations play a role in policy-making at the highest level.

A number of political irritants exist in Western relations with Russia. In arms transfers, these include: Russian accusations that the US and other Western nations are deliberately excluding Russia from its 'fair share' of the global arms trade; the imposition of sanctions on Russian defence enterprises because of alleged violations of Western proliferation control rules (e.g., US sanctions against Glavkosmos for its sale of cryogenic engines to India); and, the considerable sales success of Western arms-exporting nations (e.g., the US, the UK, France and Germany) relative to the massive decline in Russian exports. This situation is fraught with misunderstandings and divergences of economic interest. For reasons already examined, it is unlikely that Western nations will respond positively to complaints that they are 'being unfair' to Russia in not helping it to sell arms overseas. Indeed, the naivety displayed by Russian complaints is as exasperating as it is surprising, given Russia's own use of its weapons to reduce its international debt with its former allies in Eastern Europe.[38]

Because the transfers of process and factory production technologies are used as 'sweeteners' in arms negotiations, Russia may seek to sell its production expertise as a way to gain access to currently closed markets. Recent aircraft sales to China have seen the transfer of Su-27 aircraft production facilities and technical assistance.[39] In addition, the sale of SA-10 (S-300) surface-to-air missiles (SAM) has also seen the transfer of production facilities and maintenance assistance. Russian defence enterprises have recently shown a willingness to depart from cash-based arms transfers, in favour of complex counter-trade arrangements. Because of the parallel fall in domestic orders, Russia is increasingly keen to sell advanced weapons in order to lower the unit costs of these items. Russia has proved to be vulnerable to the same cost pressures that afflict Western arms producers, as evidenced by the feverish activity of Russian defence enterprises at global arms expositions such as those held in Dubai and Singapore. Systems previously unknown to Western intelligence agencies such as the R-73 (AA-11) air-to-air missile are now appearing for sale to developing world clients.[40] The fact that these systems are now available for export *prior to their domestic procurement* is indicative of the new situation.[41] In order to capture external markets, Russia is increasingly willing to break old patterns of arms supply, and compete in technology transfers as a means of ensuring minimal market share.

In addition, there is now a lively upgrade market for previously exported Soviet aircraft and land armoured vehicles. Follow-on upgrades are available from a number of different sources. In addition to Russia and Ukraine, France, Israel, Hungary and the Czech Republic are all marketing sub-system upgrades for aircraft such as the MiG-23 and Su-17.[42]

As well as the growing upgrade market, existing inventories and surplus industrial capacity present an almost irresistible source of foreign-currency earnings for defence producers in the CIS and Eastern Europe. In recent months Russia, for example, has used debt-for-arms swaps as a means of reducing its foreign debt. Russia exchanged MiG-29s for approximately $1 billion in foreign debts owed to Hungary. In those countries already operating a number of Soviet systems in their national arsenals (e.g., India), arms supplied on a concessional basis can also fill critical spare parts shortages. Russia has tried to negotiate agreements with its former customers for just such resupply relationships, thus far with little success. Many of Russia's traditional customers view it as an unreliable supplier due to internal political unrest.

Conversion imperatives in the Russian defence–industrial complex has forced individual enterprises to fight for survival. The ineffectiveness of centralised conversion programmes, and the relative inefficiency of government export promotion, has created the potential for entrepreneurship in foreign defence sales. Faced with declining domestic orders and the end of governmental subsidies, these firms are increasingly left to plan their own restructuring and future economic prospects. Privatisation initiatives launched by the Russian government have thus far not been successful. The broader market transition of the Russian economy impedes the adoption of radical restructuring campaigns in defence industries. As a short-cut to financing industrial restructuring, export sales are, therefore, an attractive option.

Russian defence exporters are facing a loss of traditional markets in East-Central Europe, and a limited market in the developing world. Concerns with supplier reliability will impair Russian export competitiveness for the foreseeable future. Upgrade markets provide a potential way out for individual enterprises, but foreign competition will also inhibit export success. Joint ventures between Western firms and defence enterprises in Russia are a potentially profitable avenue in these cases. Preliminary negotiations of this kind have already taken place, though large-scale contracts have not been signed.[43]

Technology diffusion in the global arms trade is thus significantly affected by second-tier suppliers, who complicate the picture of defence exports considerably. The aggregate effects of these new defence producers may be summarised as follows:

Second-tier technology sources exacerbate the breakdown of old supplier networks;
Diversification strategies in recipient countries are designed to reduce the influence of primary suppliers, and to increase indigenisation of technologies through offsets and countertrade;
A significant upgrade market exists, where Russian and other CIS defence producers are seeking to protect their productive bases through joint ventures with Western firms;
The shape of the technology transfer setting will be critically influenced by the longer-term success or failure of Russian defence exports.

The breakdown of older supplier networks means that supply-side control of recipients through arms transfers is becoming less feasible. In the face of the diversification strategies adopted by recipients, the principal suppliers are unlikely to exercise tight control over technology diffusion in offset and licensed production arrangements. Diversification strategies will in turn accelerate technology diffusion by increasing the economic viability of niche (second-tier) suppliers of defence products. Because of the lesser skills of second-tier producers, their energies are likely to be diverted towards sub-system and upgrade markets, which also require a smaller initial investment than would a full-scale advanced weapons production capability. Comprehensive design and systems integration skills take time to develop. It is likely that these skills can be acquired – or borrowed – through joint ventures between second-tier firms and multinational companies from the advanced industrial countries.

Market research has revealed that upgrade markets for aircraft and other advanced systems may well exceed the requirements for *new* systems by the year 2000. Russian arms exports have the potential to affect each of the four trends deriving from second-tier defence exports. Finally, the Russian government may seek actively to assist its firms because of the unique contribution that defence exports could make to industrial restructuring. The Russian government may choose to act because: defence exports are probably the most reliable source of foreign exchange (even if success is not assured); and exports help to protect the integrity of the Russian defence industrial base, something considered critical to national security. Russia probably retains its old interest in using arms transfers to cultivate political influence. The direction of its export policies is now influenced by a desire for access to Western technologies and joint venture activities. This, in turn, may moderate Russian export behaviour. Domestic political imperatives variously reinforce and inhibit this tendency, as foreign arms suppliers continue to sign lucrative deals with arms purchasers. The balance of interest lies between improved relations with the West, and the availability of arms markets in the developing world. As these markets continue to subside, perhaps Russia will be inclined to police its arms sales more rigorously.

Non-proliferation policy and linkage politics
Export controls carry both costs and benefits. The acceptable balance between enforcement costs and security is a function of the strength of international agreement on controls, and the distribution of costs borne by suppliers and recipients. These countries share an interest in expanding international trade. The economic interest is balanced by the more diffuse joint concern with the spread of advanced weapon technologies to states who intend to use them to change their relations with their neighbours through intimidation, or the use of military force. Because international trade in dual-use technologies is a growing area, proliferation risks and economic growth concerns dove-tail with one another. Unfortunately, measures taken to ensure technology security may disadvantage the recipients, and inhibit market growth for suppliers. This leads to disagreement among states (and analysts) over the relative efficacy of technology export controls, and to controversy over the real economic costs of transfer restrictions.

Because end-use certification of dual-use technologies is inherently imperfect, a proliferation risk exists in the trade in these items. The seriousness of the risk of diversion – that is, the diffusion of dual-use technologies from permissible to illicit uses – must be assessed against the level of consensus against proscribed uses. More narrowly, the link between traditional non-proliferation concerns and dual-use technologies lies in their importance in programmes for developing weapons of mass destruction. Dual-use items such as inertial guidance systems, rocket motors, metal-bending equipment and numerical machine tools for fine milling work all have applications in ballistic-missile development programmes. Parallel uses for these items include the development of a commercial space launch vehicle, the establishment of specialty manufacturing facilities for aerospace and engineering uses, and the manufacture of drilling equipment.[44]

To address this issue adequately, it is necessary to focus on two examples of proliferation control regimes which deal with contrasting aspects of the problem. Of particular importance in this regard are the Nuclear Non-Proliferation Treaty (NPT) and the Chemical Weapons Convention (CWC). The details of the particular treaties are beyond the scope of this paper, but two characteristics of the regimes are of importance. First, the NPT creates two classes of states, nuclear weapons states (NWS) and non-nuclear weapons states (NNWS). The NWS agree not to transfer nuclear weapons to NNWS, while at the same time assisting them in peaceful applications of nuclear technology.[45] In addition, the NWS pledge to give their best efforts to the pursuit of nuclear disarmament. NNWS agree not to develop, or seek the transfer of, nuclear weapons from the NWS. At the same time, the benefits that NNWS states receive are diffuse – that is, they are not clearly specified in terms of timeliness or proportionality.

Under the CWC, however, a universal prohibition is established on the possession and development of chemical weapons. The Convention has established an Organisation for the Prohibition of Chemical Weapons (OPCW), and implements intrusive verification procedures to ensure the destruction of weapons stocks and precursor chemicals by its signatories. Because both suppliers and recipients under the CWC are giving up proscribed items, there is a rough symmetry over the rights and responsibilities of 'weapons states' (current holders), and 'non-weapons states'. Correspondingly, there is probably less potential in this regime for disagreements between the 'haves' and 'have-nots', compared with the NPT.[46]

The situation regarding dual-use technologies resembles that of the NPT, in that supplier responsibilities and recipient benefits differ, due to the rights of NWS (suppliers) to make use of proscribed technologies in ways prohibited to NNWS (recipients). In political terms, supplier responsibilities and recipient benefits also differ, in that suppliers have control over both research and applications in dual-use areas, while recipients must comply with supplier rules or face embargo. The CWC model is interesting because it indicates that it is possible for suppliers and recipients to agree on a mutually restraining regime with roughly symmetrical rights and responsibilities.[47]

A second link also exists between suppliers and recipients in dual-use areas: that between conventional armaments and the prohibition of weapons of mass destruction. Under the NPT, developing states agree to refrain from acquiring 'defensive' weapons available to protect their national security. A tacit *quid pro quo* existed (and continues to exist) between the prohibition of weapons of mass destruction and the continuing availability of conventional armaments. Indeed, the size of the conventional arms market since the 1968 NPT indicates the continuing commitment of the leading arms suppliers (the NWS) to maintain the supply of conventional arms to developing countries. In recent years, however, this tacit bargain has begun to unravel, most apparently in the area of dual-use technologies. Inherently multiple-use, with inadequate certification of end-use applications, dual-use technologies challenge the bases of conventional non-proliferation thinking. At the same time, the shift in bargaining power between suppliers and recipients discussed in Chapter I coincides with an increasingly asymmetrical supplier–recipient relationship resembling that of the NPT. This fact further undermines the potential for institution-building in the dual-use area, and impedes the expansion of existing regimes.

Regimes such as the MTCR and Cocom which seek to expand their membership must address the asymmetry between supplier and recipient rights. At the very least, modifications to a denial-based policy to include some positive incentives (for recipients) to comply would help partially to redress the balance. The contemporary 'buyers' market that exists for arms and dual-use technology will make itself felt in this area. Recipients will simply not agree to arms-transfer arrangements which inhibit their continuing access to support technologies in a defined weapons area. In turn, as observed elsewhere in this discussion, supplying states concerned with market share are unlikely to insist upon new restrictions for their principal customers.

The diversification strategies of arms-transfer recipients increase their bargaining power over developed states in arms-transfer negotiations. In dual-use technologies essential to advanced weapons systems, developing countries can credibly argue that their continuing access to peaceful applications should not be infringed. The developed world's concern with proliferation thus makes it a hostage to the compliance behaviour of recipient states. Regulations on technology transfer must correspondingly be designed to minimise the incentives to cheat on whatever dual-use restrictions are agreed. The economic and techno-logical environment is simply too favourable to recipients for punitive measures to work.

III. TOWARDS SUPPLY-SIDE MANAGEMENT OF THE ARMS TRADE

The political and economic setting of the arms trade is hostile to increased international regulation. The economic and institutional impact of existing supplier groups also makes expansion of their membership difficult. Proliferation control objectives must still be addressed, however. The spread of weapons of mass destruction continues to concern policy-makers worldwide. Where the attention of policy-makers turns to delivery vehicles for weapons of mass destruction, or to increasingly destructive conventional arms in regions of ongoing conflict, proliferation control objectives necessarily focus on conventional arms. Supplier groups, which are basically little more than supplier cartels, are hampered in their response to new problems by their limited membership. Clearly, expansion of this membership is the first step towards enhancing international responses to proliferation problems. There are, however, serious impediments to achieving this in the near term.

The second factor that offends developing states is the focus on the denial of dual-use technologies to 'problem' countries. Transparency enhancement measures (e.g., open reporting of technology trade, relatively unambiguous export-control regulations, and rigorous but achievable systems of end-use certification) offer ways around this problem, but only if suppliers and recipients are both involved in determining the information necessary to ensure against violations.

Second-tier producers of dual-use technologies are the very countries which the established supplier groups wish to integrate as new members. A step towards this end would be to modify, and where possible remove, restrictions on technology exports to countries which possess basic technical capabilities in the proscribed area, or which enjoy access to 'third-country' sources for controlled items. Mature or obsolescent technologies also present a problem for proliferation control policies. Iraq's use of calutrons for uranium enrichment shows the potential for a 50-year old technology to enable proliferators to circumvent restrictive controls designed to inhibit the application of more modern technologies to weapons production. Policy responses to this problem confront a diverse and information-rich technical environment. The spread of scientific and engineering expertise during the last five decades ensures that attempts to limit particular applications will always face an uphill battle. Nevertheless, as circumvention in particular areas is discovered, special responses should be considered – even if they go no further than enhanced surveillance of patterns of end-use.

In the arms trade the major suppliers still represent well over 80% of the global market. As a result, second-tier producers are unlikely to consider restraint in the absence of prior moves by the market leaders. In particular cases of ongoing conflict, however, the UN has shown itself willing to consider selective embargoes. Thus, some political dialogue on the impact of transferred weapons does take place, although seldom separate from discussions on the resolution of specific conflicts. No general agreement exists concerning which weapons are destabilising, beyond that covering weapons of mass destruction. As such, a framework that closely imitates the NPT or the CWC in an attempt to prohibit entire classes of conventional weapons is unlikely to succeed. Nevertheless, a departure from pure technology denial policies could reopen some aspects of the political debate on conventional arms transfer restraint.

Technology denial and positive incentives
While highly institutionalised restraints on arms transfers are unlikely, there continues to be development at the national level in the dual-use area. In the United States in particular, there are moves to loosen regulations governing most dual-use items, instead concentrating on a small list of more closely regulated weapons-specific items.[1] This, of course, begs the question of which items constitute 'weapons-specific' technologies. There is widespread disagreement on this issue both between and within countries. Controversies surrounding the deregulation of computer technologies, the release of numerically controlled machine tools and telecommunications equipment all exemplify the increasing difficulty of differentiating weapons technologies from those which are inherently dual-use. Added to this problem is the lack of developed, rigorous control methodologies appropriate to dual-use technologies. Complex licensing and end-use certification procedures seriously inhibit legitimate international trade. Domestic economic interests argue that, where multiple sources exist, little is to be gained from unilateral restraint on sales. The argument over the contrasting decision-making imperatives of commercial firms and governments thus returns to centre-stage.

Suppliers and recipients view the issue of technology and arms-transfer regulation from opposite positions. For suppliers, market competition means that unilateral measures inhibiting sales represent little more than economic losses. For recipients, impediments on access to 'legitimate' arms and dual-use technologies constitute discrimination by developed countries. Except in particular cases, where transfers embarrass or threaten the interests of both supplier and recipient governments, coordination of policies between the two sides is difficult to envisage. Nevertheless, most arms sales – and a good deal of dual-use technology trade – takes place in areas where both suppliers and recipients enjoy converging economic (if not political) interests. Whether confined to trade expansion, or more traditional geostrategic rationales, arms transfers retain considerable political content. Focusing on issues where supplier and recipient interests converge is therefore the first step towards multilateral policy-making in this area.

Disputes among suppliers regarding restrictions on arms transfers frequently occur over the advisability of selling arms to 'rogue' states. Competition among suppliers ensures that the definition of a rogue state is inherently difficult to pin down. Countries which have seen the collapse of their export markets in recent years – namely Russia and countries in East-Central Europe – are particularly prone to a broad reading of the international consensus against transfers to dangerous nations.[2] Further, because of harsh market conditions, the weak political consensus among suppliers regarding tacit transfer restrictions is vulnerable to attack from groups within supplier countries themselves. Indeed, alliances in domestic political debates between arms-control advocates and those who favour high domestic defence spending can impede the reform of export controls to take account of a rapidly changing supply-side situation.[3] The expansion of supplier groups is argued by some to mean a reduction in export controls coverage, thereby increasing the prospect of proliferation. Such charges overstate the success of existing export controls, and undervalue the strength of underlying changes in supply networks in the arms trade. Nevertheless, these charges offer potent political weapons for those suspicious of departures in arms export-control policy.

Major supplier organisations such as the MTCR and the NSG must have a membership that reflects the changing distribution of technological capabilities in the world. This means that states that are currently targets of some form of technology access restriction will be asked in the future to participate in restrictive multilateral policies. The bargaining that will take place between these two groups (established supplier groups and third-country sources of proscribed technologies) will be intensely political and difficult. An example of such discussions was provided recently by the Cocom Coordination Forum, in which former WTO nations met with NATO members to discuss the political and administrative actions necessary to set up new national export controls based on the Cocom model. In turn, bargaining between Western nations and Russia in the context of the creation of

Cocom's successor is both lengthy and complex, necessitating compromises in both controlled items lists and proscribed destinations.[4]

RECIPIENT CONCERNS

While the inclusion of second-tier suppliers in established institutions is a worthy goal, it is insufficient by itself to satisfy recipients' concerns that their interests are being considered adequately in any broad system of arms-transfer regulation. Existing supplier groups must address the evolving diversification strategies followed by recipients as they seek to ensure access to restricted technologies by exploiting multiple sources of proscribed items. However, the pursuit of less restricted access does not by itself mean that a particular state is seeking the most advanced (or threatening) weapons. Restrictions target broad technology acquisition without effectively discriminating between those countries which are intent on acquiring advanced weapons *at all costs*, and those which are less committed to an expensive and long-term arms-acquisition strategy. This difference is key to assessing the risk of proliferation represented by technology transfer trends. If opportunistic, *ad hoc* acquisition strategies are the norm, then policies should be directed towards the provision of legitimate weapons requirements and political confidence-building between neighbours. If, however, acquisition efforts are more broad-based, with a regime identifying its sovereignty and independence with non-adherence to international norms on weapons possession, then a different policy is in order. Iraq is a good example of the latter case, while Brazil and Argentina are good examples of the former.[5]

With opportunistic states, diversification strategies present an opportunity for a *quid pro quo* on restrictions. In return for adherence to multilateral restrictions on end-use, access can be provided to developmentally important dual-use items. In the case of conventional arms, guaranteed resupply and involvement in the arms industries of the leading supplier can be powerful incentives for recipient collaboration in arms-transfer regulations. Competition between suppliers threatens to undo this potential restraining factor, however, encouraging instead the diversification of supply-linkages by recipients for economic gain, with few, if any, suppliers showing an awareness of the longer-term consequences of their marketing efforts.

The spread of industrial offsets and licensed production in arms transfers means that economic and political rationales for sales become mutually reinforcing. Arguments in favour of restraint thus face an additional hurdle as the economic benefits promised to recipients become more and more lucrative.[6] Recipient states are highly sophisticated in their bargaining in this area, increasingly favouring indirect offsets that contribute to their overall level of economic and technical development. Saudi Arabia has been particularly successful in achieving complex and far-reaching agreements with UK and US defence firms. These agreements involve Western firms guaranteeing that the Saudi economy receives an agreed level of benefits in each arms acquisition. These benefits involve commitments to invest in Saudi industry, the purchase of goods from local suppliers, and the establishment of joint ventures. The 'payout' period of these agreements frequently exceeds the life of the arms acquisitions themselves, thus ensuring the continuing contribution of technical investments to the Saudi economy (see Figure 1). More generally, the spread of complex offset agreements in the arms trade exemplifies two contrasting recipient views on supply diversification.

First, direct offset agreements integrate the recipient of arms and dual-use technologies into the productive base of the supplier. While this may actually increase the dependence of a recipient on an arms supplier, the convergence of technical standards in weapons – itself a result of competition in the arms trade – partially minimises this danger.

Second, indirect offsets contribute to the more general economic welfare of recipients. These benefit packages – in conjunction with diversification strategies allowing the linkage of offset joint ventures – represent a deepening of fundamental technical ties with supplier nations. As *Jane's Defence Weekly* concluded in an analysis of Saudi Arabian offset policy:

> The positive side of these various international offset arrangements is that an increasing degree of technological cross-meshing of lateral and vertical integration is occurring between programmes. For instance, in an approved Al Yamamah offset proposal, Rolls-Royce is joining the Middle East Propulsion Company (a civil/military jet engine repair and overhaul facility) established under the Peace Shield offsets arrangement [with the US]. In addition, AEC, another Peace Shield offspring, is producing UK subsystems for US-produced weapons platforms, and is seeking to expand its electronics work through possible Al Yamamah subcontracting.[7]

Over the longer-term, such links may help a developing state to improve its position in the international economy.

Figure 1: Al Yamamah (Saudi Arabia) Economic Offset Proposals[8]

Company	Project	Status
BAe/Dowty/Hughes	Repair and maintenance of missiles	Approved
BAe	ALUSA smelter project	Not yet approved
Royal Ordnance	Military–industrial project	Not yet approved
Various companies	Technical training centres	Approved
Various companies	Production of agricultural/ horticultural netting using oil feedstock	Withdrawn
Rolls-Royce	Manufacture of acrylic products using local oil-derived feedstock	Withdrawn
BAe (Dandsk BIOprotein)	Production of food additives for livestock and fish farms	Not yet approved
BAe/Leyland DAF	Production of military vehicles	Withdrawn
Copperheat International	Contract service using latest heat treatment technology	Withdrawn
Booker Tate	Processing oil seeds for animal feed	Approved
Glaxo	Production of ethical pharmaceuticals, including Zantac and Ventolin	Approved
BAe/Technomaiera	Production of lightweight marble and granite	Approved
BAe Vanderlande Industries	Production of materials handling systems	Approved
BAe/Culligan Italiana	Production of water treatment products and installations	Proposed
Tate & Lyle/Sarola	Sugar refinery	Not yet approved
BAe/Bibby Sterilin	Disposable plasticware	Withdrawn

A similar – although slightly less onerous offset policy, is that of the UAE. The Emirates insist that foreign defence contractors establish a proportional offset of up to 4% of the value of weapons acquisitions. Defence firms must invest this amount in local businesses. Because the UAE intends to spend over $2bn a year for the next five years on foreign arms acquisitions, this investment requirement should provide considerable assistance to new local businesses. Domestic UAE considerations drove the design of this policy. As *Jane's Defence Weekly* observes, declining oil prices meant that large arms acquisitions would have conflicted with domestic infrastructure investments:

> The fledgeling UAE Offset Group was created to solve a dilemma of increased demands for spending in the welfare and military sectors while the price of oil was low, said Al-Din. For the UAE to have entered into a procurement programme would have taken capital away from areas such as education.[9]

Similar concerns are visible in Malaysia, where the acquisition of MiG-29 and F/A-18 aircraft from Russia and the United States respectively, has triggered negotiations on direct offset benefits to the local economy. For example, Malaysian firms will produce Swiss MD3-160 trainers under licence from British Aerospace. This programme is related to the prior sale of *Hawk* trainer aircraft by BAe to the Malaysian government.[10] Russia is negotiating with Malaysia to co-produce and sell aircraft spares in the Asia-Pacific region. This more aggressive pursuit of export business is itself tied to an institutional shift in Russia which saw the creation of Rosvoorouzhenie – the state military equipment export organisation – which itself replaced three separate organisations left over from the old Soviet regime.[11] Together, these events illustrate the complementary supply- and demand-side adjustments which are part of the increasingly global defence marketplace. They also indicate the wide-ranging effects of recipient market power on the nature of arms transfer relationships.

In a situation characterised by multiple arms and dual-use technology suppliers and overlapping offset agreements, recipient diversification strategies achieve a number of complementary goals:

> Ensuring against the failure of some offset agreements to deliver promised benefits;

> Capturing foreign equity investments in joint venture firms established locally; in this case a subsidiary may become an integral part of the parent firm.

Fostering technology transfer through the freer distribution of intellectual property in intra-firm contacts within joint ventures.

Offset packages thus offer a model of how to accomplish positive technology transfer. Incentives, designed as packages of 'withholdable benefits', may influence recipients to collaborate with multilateral efforts to control the arms trade, particularly if implemented in consultation with established supplier groups. The addition of positive incentives to traditional embargo-based approaches would at least break open the mutually reinforcing character of export trends currently dominating the arms trade. More narrowly, then, eschewing an institutionally complex and politically infeasible system of multilateral restrictions on arms transfers, a more limited policy coordination initiative might emphasise the broad principles outlined in the next sections.

AN INCENTIVES-BASED APPROACH TO ARMS AND DUAL-USE TECHNOLOGY TRANSFER REGULATION

- Such an approach must be centred on established supplier organisations, and emphasise informal policy coordination implemented through the agreements (Memoranda of Understanding) which already structure relations between suppliers and arms transfer recipients;

- Arms-transfer agreements should emphasise indirect offsets, rather than benefits which expand the industrial overcapacity of global arms industries. In this way, contributions to economic development flowing from arms acquisitions contribute less to export incentives in the global arms trade;

- Political links must be associated in some way with arms transfers. Weapons are not the same as other internationally traded commodities and should not be subject to the same treatment as ordinary commercial items;

- Regulated access to stabilising weapons technologies should be guaranteed to all who commit themselves to a broad initiative aimed at regulating multilateral arms transfers. The nature of destabilising technologies should be determined by existing supplier groups and established treaty regimes regulating the spread of weapons of mass destruction;

- End-use certification in transferred weapon and dual-use technologies should be based on a system of reciprocal information sharing. Two proposals which exemplify this principle are the UN Arms

48

Transfer Register, and the post-Cocom proposal for pre-delivery consultations on arms transfers among the leading suppliers;

• Suppliers should agree to link their offset packages, allowing for the pooling of offset benefits to underwrite particular regional security agreements and conflict resolution efforts.[12]

Current political and economic conditions offer a significant barrier to new institution-building in the regulation of arms transfers. The approach highlighted above depends only upon informal policy coordination efforts, with a premium on the leadership of the only state that has thus far identified proliferation as the most significant threat to its national security – the United States. While Western European and Russian collaboration is important, that of the United States is essential since it is the only country which has the potential to dominate any part of the arms market that it chooses to enter.[13] This market power is a significant lever which, if used judiciously, might encourage the collaboration of many other suppliers in multilateral sales restraint. This influence is, however, a wasting asset. In the case of the Russian Federation, for instance, policies which linked conversion assistance to collaboration on export restraint might have proved effective two years ago, but would be much more difficult to implement today.[14] In turn, the current period of international defence industry adjustment offers a closing window of opportunity for the multilateral coordination of restraint.[15] If industrial readjustment policies can be crafted in coordination with more restrained export-promotion programmes, longer-term agreement on arms transfer control will be easier to achieve. The basic argument is that less export-oriented industries, alongside more restrained arms-transfer policies by governments, will lay the groundwork for a more serious institutionally based attempt at conventional proliferation control in the future.[16] Without these preliminary measures, however, further progress in this area is unlikely to be achieved. Adopting policies in accordance with evolving market conditions offers the best opportunity for more far-reaching policy goals in the medium-to-long term.

Concerns with discrimination in arms and dual-use controls are addressed through a basic shift in emphasis in the regulation of technology flows. Instead of focusing on supplier-recipient pairs, regulatory efforts would address the participation or non-participation of states in a political bargain designed to ensure stable and (more-or-less) non-controversial access to conventional arms. Such a shift in emphasis has a number of implications for the broader issue of supply management in the global arms trade.

An approach to regulating arms transfers which centres on supplier groups would increase the rule-governed character of the arms trade. It would channel economic forces in a direction that assists, rather than confronts, trends in technology diffusion. Economic incentives could continue to determine national participation in lucrative arms-transfer agreements; however, under the initiatives proposed above, regulatory efforts would be focused on a predetermined pledge to provide offset benefits of a defined nature over an agreed period. Different defence industry consortia could (as they do now) compete with one another in offering creatively designed offset packages with a given financial value. The difference in this approach is that commercial negotiations would be part of a political process designed to enhance transparency and confidence-building in arms transfers.

A second feature of this approach is the transferability of offset benefits within an overall regulatory regime. In brief, if a counterpart fund were set up by participating nations to some level (for example, the average annual income stream gained from the defence exports of the average of the five largest exporting firms), offset benefits could be made convertible (that is, insurable) in a way that supported the economic viability of what is in any case an example of market sharing. Such an initiative would have two critical strengths. First, it could serve as a form of insurance for defence firms against the business risk that they incur in multi-year indirect offset commitments. Second, some portion of the fund could be made refundable in hard currency for both suppliers *and* recipients. This would allow suppliers who have voiced an interest in defence conversion (for example, in Russia and Ukraine) to receive financial assistance towards that end.

This plan would also allow Russia to participate in the offset segment of arms transfer competition, and would thereby negate part of the impetus to export increasingly sophisticated arms as a means of gaining market share. This initiative thus offers the former Soviet Union the potential for stabilising its market presence and gaining financial assistance for defence conversion. Over the longer term, such an approach might significantly alter the export orientation of Russian defence enterprises.[17]

Confidence-building measures and transparency in arms sales
The previous section offered a selection of initiatives aimed at increasing the regulation of international arms transfers. A critical parallel development is the need to increase the transparency of arms and dual-use trade. The first significant move in this direction is the UN Arms Transfer Register. The first year of the Register was especially en-

couraging because new information was introduced into the public debate on arms transfers. In addition, a higher level of participation than expected was achieved. Significant improvements in the Register will be required, however, if it is to increase its relevance to broader efforts at regulating international arms transfers.

First, the Register needs to reform its seven reporting categories. At present, the categories (Battle Tanks, Armoured Combat Vehicles, Large Calibre Artillery Systems, Combat Aircraft, Attack Helicopters, Warships, and Missiles and Missile Launchers) are of limited usefulness in examining the structure of import patterns.[18] Similarly, the absence of a requirement to report weapons type within each category means that issues such as the age of an existing inventory – which place new acquisitions in an important light – are hidden from the observer. The need to include a greater level of information in the Register will face political obstacles from both suppliers and recipients. However, if the Register is to evolve any further, it must confront at least some of these issues in order to expand the embryonic consensus behind restrictions on the free flow of arms.

An additional characteristic of the Register is the provision of background information on military holdings, weapons development programmes and defence expenditures. A trial exercise was attempted in the first Register report, with 9 of the 23 governments involved in the UN Group of Technical Experts participating. Malcolm Chalmers and Owen Greene point out the apparent difficulties that states had in providing the requested data:

> Out of 23 governments represented in the Group, nine provided background information on procurement and holdings last year, and these are likely to support the regularisation of this data in the annual published Register. Non-inclusion of background data does not necessarily indicate opposition to Register expansion, and a number of the remaining countries have expressed their support for the inclusion of holdings and procurement in the main part of the Register. That so many Governments have so far been unable to provide any background information in this regard, however, makes it difficult to predict the outcome of the 1994 Group's deliberations on this central agenda item.[19]

If significant difficulties accompany the provision of background information by the sponsors of the seven-category register, one can only wonder at the problems that would arise if more detailed information were to be required from others. It seems clear, however, that if the Register were part of a broader regulatory initiative, participating states might have a more positive attitude towards its information reporting function. Coverage, for instance, of the value of direct and indirect offsets in arms transfers would add an important new aspect to the Register's role.

The political limitations of the UN Arms Transfer Register are illustrative of the difficulties of achieving real progress in regulating arms sales. Procedural difficulties associated with the Register can be summarised as follows: the absence of secretariat follow-up in the case of reporting anomalies; the obsessive secrecy that still afflicts much of the global arms trade; and the political impossibility of UN-sponsored analysis of destabilising arms flows. Each of these weaknesses indicates that the Register is in need of political assistance from like-minded governments. That assistance only appears likely if one of two things occurs – either the political barriers to the Register's deepening are overcome, or a parallel system of transparency enhancement and supply management is instituted. Only if an economic or political interest in greater transparency is created will states change their lukewarm attitude towards arms transfer surveillance.

The general approach outlined in this chapter aims at addressing the reasons why second-tier participation in arms transfer restraint is unlikely. Supplier organisations must change in order for these new countries to join. Incentives to participate must derive from positive political (and hopefully economic) interests. No haranguing on moral grounds is likely to sway governments. Such arguments seldom work in the developed world, and are unlikely to be more persuasive elsewhere.

Compliance and supply management in arms transfers
Supply management offers a coordinated approach to regulating the trade in arms and dual-use technologies. This approach attempts to work *with* the evolving economics of global arms markets, rather than against them. In short, supply management offers a means of coordinating responses to the industrial problems faced by suppliers, while at the same time attempting to control the diffusion of increasingly sophisticated conventional weapons. This is a transitional strategy. Negative conditions in the contemporary global market are a considerable obstacle to new attempts to regulate arms transfers. The existing institutions created by suppliers during the Cold War must also be taken into account. These groups are necessarily the core of any new approach to regulating technology transfers, and, unfortunately, also the central obstacle to new thinking in proliferation control.

Supplier groups as currently constituted have exclusive memberships, and are analogous to commercial cartels. This fact has both positive and negative aspects. First, groups such as the MTCR and formerly Cocom have experience in the design of surveillance systems for policing restricted technologies. Supplier groups have also coordinated national export guidelines for decades. Cocom, for example, used to operate a multilateral framework of controls with approximately 30 permanent staff in the US Embassy in Paris. This small coordination mechanism is in stark contrast to the considerable legal and surveillance assets used to control restricted technology transfers at the national level. The costs of regulation, and the compliance burden borne by business firms, are politically sensitive in most technology exporting countries. Business interests are always critical of policies which they view as limiting their freedom. In multilateral discussions on export control this leads to disputes regarding the restrictiveness and scope of regulations.

States in the former Soviet Union also have complaints concerning their access to technology transfers. Russia is the potential source of a number of cutting-edge technologies, and Russian attempts to protect its defence industrial base through exports place clear limits on its willingness to comply with international restrictions on technology transfer. However, as was observed above, if conversion – or wholesale dismantlement – of Russian defence manufacturing capacity were to take place, it is at least theoretically possible that economic pressures to export would diminish, although political rationales for exports would undoubtedly continue to be persuasive in particular cases. This does not contradict the broader point, however, that multilateral coordination of arms-transfer policies in parallel to the industrial adjustment process already under way offers the best chance for stabilising global arms markets. Supply management is the overall rubric under which a process of regulation can develop.

Second-tier arms producers – such as Brazil, Argentina and South Korea – are interested in recapturing the market share that they lost after the Iran–Iraq War. Because their industries are smaller than those of the major suppliers, these countries require smaller market opportunities to attain financial viability. The diversification strategies of arms recipients, such as the lucrative weapons upgrade contracts already appearing in the Middle East and East Asia, thus provide potential market niches for flexible second-tier arms producers. The market is being expanded further by countries with arsenals made up of weapons from the former Soviet Union. Efforts to standardise ammunition or spare parts along Western lines add to the markets opening up to these countries. The leading arms suppliers are also entering the upgrade business, and joint ventures increasingly characterise large upgrade contracts. Increases in military capability that result from upgrades of already fielded weapons raise a less visible but potentially serious proliferation concern.[20] It remains to be seen whether the leading arms exporting states are attuned to this issue, or if the search for new markets will overwhelm recommendations for caution in technology transfer.[21]

Supply management addresses concerns for market equity, protects the weakest link in the West's export controls systems (the former Soivet Union's less developed export controls), and inhibits the competitive escalation of technology content in transferred weapons systems. This approach accomplishes these goals by increasing the transparency of international defence markets, and by linking recipients to supplier groups in ways that moderate supply-side pressures for defence trade expansion. Recipient market power is a critical aspect of this new approach, and is the key difference between the Cold War arms trade and the current situation.

A supply management approach does not require abandoning negative sanctions and/or coercive measures in arms-trade regulation. It does, however, require the augmentation of these policy instruments by measures that create a positive, interest-based incentive for recipient states to participate. It is not enough to allow new members to join unaltered supplier groups. These organisations must themselves change to take account of the new characteristics of the global arms trade. The absence of a consensus on reductions in conventional arms transfers means that economic and political forces are likely to prevail over other concerns. Arms purchasers can play suppliers off against each other in pursuit of greater offset benefits and improved access to the most advanced weapons technologies.

Because conventional weapons proliferation can threaten international peace and stability, it should be a continuing concern to the major UN countries. Initiatives such as the Arms Transfer Register suggest that this fact is recognised by states. Increased transparency may at least shape the politics of arms transfers in a way that begins to build confidence between suppliers (as a group) and recipients (as a group). Diverging interests between the two sides stem from the discrimination felt by developing states, and the proliferation fears of others. Supply-side restrictions determined in the absence of broader consultations with recipients lack the legitimacy necessary to minimise the more outrageous instances of circumvention. In turn, such restrictions have demonstrably failed to constrain the ambitions of states determined to obtain weapons of mass destruction by exploiting the inevitable regulatory weaknesses of multilateral regimes.

This discussion has focused on the contribution that positive measures can make to existing supplier-oriented approaches to proliferation control. The fact remains, however, that negative sanctions play an important role in the credibility of non-proliferation regimes. The relationship between carrots and sticks in this area is a critical issue. In a supply management approach, the major sanctions-based regimes would stay in place. This is necessary because such restrictions form the backbone of a system of technology transfer which operates in an international environment of unevenly distributed technical capabilities; coercive methods play an inevitable part in multilateral proliferation control efforts. Supply management, however, means that the conception of legitimate *targets* of coercive methods differs from existing methodologies for identifying potential proliferators. Instead of supplier organisations targeting recipients in transfer restrictions, the management system would target *non-members*. This change shifts the emphasis of discrimination away from a general category of states – recipients – to specific non-participants in an open and legitimated system of weapons sales. The central gain to proliferation control is thus a dramatic increase in the transparency of arms-transfer agreements, an ongoing discussion on technology transfers between suppliers and recipients, and the more focused targeting of problem countries.

More broadly, proliferation control in conventional arms is a highly controversial policy goal. The very notion of such proliferation is contested by weapons-exporting nations. Observers of the arms trade can agree that particular transfers are a bad idea, but more general agreement on limiting the spread of conventional arms is absent. Informal discussions on supply management are analogous to early strategic arms-control efforts which focused on stabilising weapons diffusion, leaving to the future the issue of weapons dismantlement or reduced sales. By acknowledging the legitimacy of weapons transfers to independent states, a management approach avoids the first hurdle at which proposals for total disarmament usually fall: the fact that military capabilities in the world are inherently uneven. Addressing concerns regarding economic and technological offsets also adds a new set of policy instruments to assist in the greater management of dual-use technology diffusion.

Contemporary arms markets are in a state of transition. The potential exists for flooding the global market with cheap, but relatively sophisticated arms. The economic imperatives of the arms trade do not reflect political interests in a reduced level of global armament, and continued concentration on exports will further delay a necessary period of readjustment to smaller defence markets in the developed world. As such, political intervention in the global arms trade offers a means of creating some stability before the situation becomes inherently uncontrollable. Unfortunately, anticipating a threat, and preventing its emergence, is the hardest kind of policy to initiate, especially when faced with the pressure of short-term political imperatives.

CONCLUSIONS

The end of the Cold War also meant the end of a predictable and stable global arms market. In its place is emerging an increasingly complicated situation in which rapid technology diffusion is making regulation of arms and dual-use transfers ever more difficult. Supply-side competition is also creating conflicts of interest for policy-makers concerned with stemming proliferation. While the spread of conventional weapons is not subject to the same moral sanctions as the spread of weapons of mass destruction, the sale of weapons which increase the lethality and geographic scope of ongoing conflicts still generates concern. Arms-supplying countries retain an interest in fielding more advanced weapons than those they sell to developing states. Even here, however, export competition means that it is becoming increasingly necessary to export top-of-the-line systems in order to ensure market share, frequently before these items have been integrated into domestic arsenals. As a result, it is much more difficult to avoid inadvertent technology transfers, and policy concerning dual-use technologies becomes much more complicated.

The short-term predominance of economic factors in the arms trade reduces the options available to policy-makers interested in prolifera3for future policy initiatives. In the absence of improvements in this area, the confidence-building and transparency enhancement dimensions of arms control initiatives (i.e., the UN Arms Transfer Register) will be further weakened. The political difficulties which will result are many, but a few will be outlined here to give an idea of the scope of the problem.

Supplier groups such as the MTCR restrict the availability of dual-use technologies. In so doing, these groups necessarily confront developing states wishing to acquire these capabilities with two choices. First, these states can acquiesce in the international restrictions, and accept either dependent access or no access to the technologies in question. Second, however, states can seek to put together an equivalent capability from a diverse array of sources. It is here that the expansion of dual-use technology sources (see Figure 2) makes itself evident. Diversification strategies implemented by developing states have shown themselves to be effective in the covert acquisition of manufacturing and weapons technologies. The skilful manipulation of 'front' companies and off-shore investments in dual-use firms offer an effective (although undoubtedly more expensive) substitute for formal dependence upon officially known sources of dual-use technologies.

Figure 2: The Structure of the Arms Trade: The Cold War and After

International System	Cold War	Post-Cold War
Market Structure	Duopoly, with the Soviet Union leading in sales and the US second Stable supplier–recipient pairs Regulated technology access	Oligopoly, with US leadership and market fragmentation Fragmented supply networks Extensive technology transfer
Dominant Export Incentive	Political	Economic
Important Actors	The Soviet Union, the US, and the Western European industrial states	Transnational defence firms from the US and the European Union and second-tier producers
Dominant Suppliers	The US, the Soviet Union, the UK, France, China	The US, Russia, the UK, France, Germany, China
Industrial State Advantages	Stable	Unstable High-leverage counters sold by second-tier exporters Accelerating proliferation of dual-use technologies

Detecting covert supply channels of this type is becoming increasingly complicated. As technologies become more and more modular, determining the end-use (and destination) of transferred items becomes harder to accomplish. Identifying those involved in these complex technology diversion programmes is clearly a task for the intelligence services of the major suppliers. However, the resources necessary toaccomplish this task, and the increased compliance-burden borne by the legitimate trade, probably increases out of all proportion to the relative ease with which new channels for covert access can be created by recipient states. In short, the costs of regulation are likely to grow much faster than the costs to proliferators of exploiting multiple-acquisition channels for dual-use items. The political importance of compliance costs borne by business is high, especially in the context of a prolonged economic recession. How likely, then, are new intelligence resources to be allocated to address this weakness in export controls?

The recent failure of the Cocom states to reach agreement on a successor regime illustrates the seriousness of these issues. The major areas of contention seem to be a diminishing consensus on strategic restrictions on technology trade (non-weapons of mass destruction), and a refusal by some states to include a shortlist of countries in an arms embargo as a non-proliferation measure. The countries most frequently named, North Korea, Iraq, Libya and Iran, are on many lists of rogue nations. With the exception of Iran, these states are already the subject of UN or other multilateral sanctions limiting their access to transferred arms and technologies. The issue of an arms embargo against Iran now stands in the way of a broad multilateral initiative for technology transfer restrictions. Some of the states of importance to the new regime – most notably Russia – are unwilling to go along with this proposal. In turn, countries such as Germany and France simply wish the identity of targeted countries to be given a much lower public profile, arguing that 'naming names' inhibits policy flexibility by making the addition or deletion of countries from a proscribed destinations list into a public matter. These disagreements are indicative of the difficulties currently facing the coordination of export controls. A lack of consensus on basic objectives raises seemingly marginal issues to high importance, while the unwillingness of parties to sign a restrictive technology and arms transfer regime remains in the background.

The scarcity of regulatory resources has special significance when dual-use production technologies are sold through long-term arms-transfer arrangements. Production technologies spread through co-production agreements (e.g., numerically and computer controlled machine tools, and metal-bending equipment) allow developing states to increase their value-added participation in the commercial economy (see the example of Saudi Arabia in Chapter III). At the same time, the globalisation of defence industries means that additional sources and applications for these same technologies are being developed by manufacturers wishing to increase their participation in commercial trade. As commercial and defence markets converge, generic production techniques become more and more suitable for weapons fabrication. Indeed, in many areas few additional modifications (beyond software changes) are required to alter significantly the nature of a product. Clearly, the regulatory task – assuming one agrees that the production technologies of conventional weapons should be subject to transfer restrictions – is becoming more difficult. For regimes such as the MTCR (and, in a different vein, the NPT), these trends are undermining the credibility of transparency-building based on the documentation of closed cycles of equipment use and transfer. The expansion in the sources of precision manufacturing equipment is increasing the options for proliferating countries, and slowly removing control of dual-use equipment from governments and placing it in the hands of the global market place. States with access to hard currency can correspondingly purchase almost anything they desire.

An emphasis upon regulatory difficulties and compliance costs is especially important in a time of weak supplier consensus on the continuing importance of transfer restrictions. Much of the potential for progress in conventional arms transfer restrictions derives from the fact that conventional military equipment can be used as delivery vehicles for weapons of mass destruction. Much beyond this area, however, states are unwilling to constrain their weapons sales and, given the trends identified above, are unwilling to limit access to dual-use technologies. As noted in the previous chapter, the weak consensus on conventional arms transfer restraint argues against the use of institutional and regulatory approaches similar to those designed to address the spread of weapons of mass destruction. Each of the problems of regulatory cost and coherence mentioned in this discussion assumes the continuing application of basically unsuitable regulatory methods to the conventional weapons area. This is clearly the safest assumption, since institution-building in this area is becoming increasingly difficult as the Cold War consensus continues to break down.

Problems in industrial adjustment also affect the regulatory setting in arms and dual-use technologies. Commercial products with significant dual-use technology content clearly contribute to the spread of weapons-related knowledge. This has particular importance because Western defence conversion policies assume that civilian spin-on benefits to the defence sector are now more significant than the spin-off benefits of defence spending. If this belief is accurate, then globalisation in commercial technology markets – which is much greater than in the defence sector – contributes to the regulatory burden of policing process technologies as they spread to new locations. Thus industrial policies based on leveraging commercial technologies against reductions in defence R&D probably exacerbate technology security problems. Policy-makers who assume that there is an unproblematic relationship between these two areas could find themselves paradoxically achieving trade expansion at the expense of reduced technology security. The increasing difficulty of separating national security and economic policies adds to the likelihood that decisions will reflect unstable compromises which allow proliferators to circumvent weakening controls.

Defence conversion and industrial restructuring in the former Soviet Union is a critical destabilising factor in the post-Cold War arms trade. Domestic procurement in Russia and elsewhere in the former Soviet Union will undoubtedly be the predominant determinant of industry adjustment plans. In the short run, steep declines in domestic purchases have fostered reforms in export promotion and trading practices. These institutional changes help to increase the power of those constituencies in Russia which favour export expansion, and may weaken those which argue for a reduction in subsidies to military production. This is further complicated by the fact that defence enterprises in Russia are also the major source of civil products. Thus, external interventions into the allocation of resources in the Russian defence industry will require the ability to influence intra-firm decisions on investment priorities. This is a daunting exercise, and Western policy-makers lack the detailed knowledge – or ability – to intervene. But while Russian defence exports may be financially important, they are unlikely to have particular significance in longer-term resource allocations, compared to that represented by domestic procurement (and R&D subsidisation) decisions. At the same time, Western joint ventures with Russian defence firms will add to the technology content of end-products, while accelerating the commodification (or modularity) of transferred technologies. In overcoming the technical incompatibilities of Russian and Western systems, subcomponent availability will increase, thereby allowing recipients a broader menu of choices. In this same area, Western governments concerned with technology security are deliberately fostering 'turn-key' technical subsystems that can be integrated with foreign (specifically Russian) products without compromising the sensitive technical knowledge underlying their design. This meets short-run concerns about technology security by making it increasingly possible to 'mate' previously incompatible technologies (e.g., a Chinese space-launch vehicle and a US communications satellite). Developing states may, in the long term, face a smaller hurdle in acquiring 'usable' technical sub-systems while remaining in compliance with end-use certification requirements. Again, the changing relationship between compliance and transparency is confounding attempts at enhancing technology security.

Policies are especially difficult to design for conventional weapons and dual-use technologies. With no developed norms proscribing their export, regulatory practices must depend upon shared security concerns and benign economic conditions for multilateral adherence. Is it possible to build a consensus aimed at reducing technology transfers which spread conventional arms and the means of their production? Under current economic and political conditions, the answer is a resounding 'no'. If the technological environment evolves in the directions discussed above, the problem will be exacerbated, at least until the huge overcapacity in defence industries is reduced.

Even following such reduction, dual-use technologies would still present an unprecedented challenge to supply-side regulatory approaches. The industrialisation of developing countries and the globalisation of dual-use technologies mean that commercial, not political, forces determine the distribution of technical knowledge and products. Policy interventions into this economic system must account for the fact that the most that can be achieved is delay. Political objectives that seek to work against the economics of defence and dual-use trade produce unpredictable circumvention behaviour, and effectively defeat attempts to provide information on technology transfers through end-use surveillance. To break out of this cycle of increasing regulatory incapacity, parallel strategies of supply management and supplier-recipient bargaining are necessary. Supply management uses the market power of arms purchasers to reduce the pressure to increase the technology content of transferred weapons. At the same time, supply-side pressures to export would also be partially mitigated by defence industry restructuring which reduces productive overcapacity and the need to export. In this more favourable political climate, governments may be more able to forgo export opportunities.

A realistic approach to the management of arms and dual-use technology transfers must emphasise the following measures:

• Offset provisions in arms-transfer agreements should focus on *indirect* offsets which contribute to the technological development of recipient countries. Where possible, such transfers should not include weapon-production facilities, nor the ability to manufacture significant spare parts for the transferred weapons system. Such transfers only expand the capacity of global arms industries and complicate international safeguards on the re-transfer of restricted armaments.

- Multilateral export controls should focus on weapon-specific technologies in transfer restrictions, in addition to technologies important for developing weapons of mass destruction. Commercial technology applications should only be restricted where significant 'third country' sources for controlled items do not exist. The economic costs of broad export controls are too significant to allow for a generalised embargo on technology transfers.

- Enhanced end-use certification of dual-use transfers should be established to increase the transparency of Third World mixed industrial strategies. Administrative and technical assistance in establishing export-control systems should be granted to developing countries in return for the de-targeting of their industries by Western export laws.

- Supplier groups should be expanded to include all major sources of conventional arms and dual-use technologies. In addition, Third World countries should be integrated into supplier groups through a multilateral dialogue on technology restrictions. This could be furthered by de-targeting proscribed destinations in export controls in return for those countries agreeing to modify their technology export behaviour.

In the absence of such measures, it is unlikely that conventional weapons proliferation control will become anything more than a controversial analytical concept.

APPENDIX: MAJOR SUPPLIER ORGANISATIONS

The major supplier organisations implement their regulations through national legislation. Coordination of national regulations takes place through information sharing and *ad hoc* decision-making. International controls items lists mediate differences in national export controls. Differences in these frameworks are the subject of diplomatic bargaining.

The Missile Technology Control Regime

The MTCR was created in April 1987 by the G-7 group of countries. It was designed to restrain the spread of ballistic- and cruise-missile technologies to developing countries. In its original incarnation, the regime was aimed at limiting delivery vehicles capable of launching nuclear weapons over medium-to-long range distances. This criterion was embodied in the range-payload index of 300km and 500kg that formed the basis of the two-category regulatory framework. Category I items are ballistic and cruise missiles with the designated range-payload capabilities, production facilities for these systems, and associated support equipment. Category II items are dual-use missile technology and components as well as major subcomponents of Category I items, such as missile-guidance systems, precursors for solid rocket fuel (e.g., fuel binders), and rocket motors.[1] The MTCR is not a treaty, and thus its policy coordination functions do not create legally binding obligations to restrict transfers. Nevertheless, the regime has gained credibility from its importance in inhibiting at least two missile-acquisition programmes in the developing world: the abortive Condor II project involving Iraq, Egypt and Argentina; and the short-lived sale of cryogenic engines and technology from Glavkosmos of Russia to the Indian Space Research Organisation (ISRO). In neither case were the transfers completed as originally intended. It is equally important to note, however, that related technologies still diffused to each of these countries, sometimes from countries who are members of the regime.[2]

The MTCR has now expanded to 25 members, and has altered its category system to include launch vehicles designed to deliver other unconventional munitions, namely chemical and biological weapons. This change effectively brings whole new classes of missiles within the regime's purview due to the different masses (payload sizes) characteristic of the additional weapons types, something which may test the commitment of some regime members to the evolving non-proliferation norm in this area. In turn, there is only limited agreement in the developing world on the 'weapons of mass destruction' character of surface-to-surface missiles. The notion that these weapons constitute a part of a 'poor man's A-bomb' carries some resonance for countries like North Korea and Pakistan. Equally, the diffusion of space-launch vehicle technology inherently limits any restrictions on the diffusion of missile-related subsystems.

Unilateral additions to the MTCR restrictions are also a part of the aggregate missile control regime. The United States in particular has adopted a highly restrictive interpretation of missile proliferation, which uses economic viability criteria to assess whether space-launch vehicle programmes in the developing world have a covert weapons purpose. In addition, the US has adopted a case-by-case policy on transfers of missile technology, alongside a policy of presumptive denial – *even when regime members are involved*. It is unclear to what extent this last policy will be fully carried out, as it would appear to constitute a significant *disincentive* for new members to join the regime. It is difficult to square this decision with the MTCR members espoused desire to shift the regime from an exclusively supplier grouping to a more inclusive organisation.

The Australia Group
Formed in 1985, the Australia Group regulates the export of dual-use chemicals and chemical technologies in order to restrict the spread of chemical weapons. Initially the organisation comprised 21 Organisation for Economic Cooperation and Development (OECD) member-states who met every six months at the Australian Embassy in Paris. These meetings were designed for the exchange of information (intelligence) on chemical weapons proliferation, and to coordinate export controls directed at developing states. The Australia Group maintains a list of 54 chemical weapons precursors which are subject to multilateral control, in addition to related chemical manufacturing technologies. In 1992 the group adopted the additional function of regulating biological organisms and toxins – and related equipment – in order to bolster the Biological Weapons Convention, a treaty lacking any enforcement or verification methodologies. Following the opening of the Chemical Weapons Convention for signature in 1993, the Australia Group must reinterpret its mandate in accordance with the voluntary restrictions on weapons holdings (complete prohibition) undertaken by participating countries. It remains to be seen whether the organisation will continue to implement regulations over and above those specified in the convention. Again, should this be the case, accusations of discrimination by developing states are a predictable result.

The Nuclear Suppliers Group

Formed in 1976 in the aftermath of the Indian 'peaceful nuclear explosion', the NSG initially comprised the US, Canada, the UK, Japan, the USSR, West Germany and France. These countries agreed to common guidelines on regulation and restraint in the transfer of civilian nuclear technologies. Although initially vague, these regulations were the first coordinated attempt by the suppliers to implement restrictions on technology transfer over and above those stipulated in the INFCIRC 66A (partial), or INFCIRC 153 (full-scope) safeguards frameworks policed by the IAEA. Because these restrictions operate in addition to those exercised within the safeguards system of the NPT, they are the subject of considerable resentment directed at the advanced industrial nations. Far from being an active cartel, the NSG did not meet between 1977 and 1991. The revelations surrounding Iraq's covert nuclear programmes provoked the group into action, however. In March 1991 the NSG agreed to re-examine prior arrangements for the surveillance of trade in nuclear dual-use items.

In April 1992, the NSG adopted restrictions on transfers of 65 categories of dual-use items. Among the equipment that is restricted under the new system are: high-strength maraging steel; beryllium; and specialised industrial equipment associated with fabricating vessels used in processing fissile material. All of these items are now subject to export licensing, with rejections of transfer requests remaining binding for three years following the negative decision. Information on unsuccessful licence requests is also to be shared among the NSG membership (now 27 states), and coordinated through the Japanese embassy in Vienna.[3]

The NSG's linkage to the NPT is crucial to its functioning, as it was designed to rectify perceived shortcomings in the NPT's policing of the civil applications of nuclear technologies. There is an inevitable tension in this relationship, however, because of the extra restrictions on transfers of technology not narrowly controlled under safeguards arrangements. Some developing countries, historically India and China, have protested at the 'rich nation's club' represented by the NSG. More importantly, India has pledged to continue its own independent nuclear development efforts even though it is targeted by the NSG as a potential proliferator. While China has recently acceded to the NPT as the last (for now) of the five nuclear weapons states, it continues to voice objections to the discriminatory application of NPT rules and obligations. This controversy requires monitoring because of the impending 1995 NPT Review and Extension Conference. During these discussions it is likely that the status of NSG restrictions on dual-use technology transfers will be raised by some developing countries. At the same time, the changing shape of the nuclear proliferation issue area mandates adaptation of the regime to the observed behaviour of proliferators – most notably that of Iraq.[4]

The Future Beyond Cocom
Negotiations among the 17 Cocom member-states began in autumn 1993 on the structure and objectives of Cocom's successor. Cocom itself ceased to exist on 31 March 1994. It was, however, extended on an *ad hoc* basis beyond this date as agreement on its successor has yet to be reached. Its successor will possess a broader membership and a changed mandate. Instead of administering a strategic embargo direct-ed against an agreed enemy, the new grouping will seek to regulate the transfer of dual-use technologies important to the spread of weapons of mass des'ruction and their delivery vehicles to potential proliferant nations. Cocom's proscribed items lists will apparently be replaced by an enhanced 'super-core' list of eight to ten technologies, which will be restricted from transfer to an agreed list of 'dangerous countries'.

Proscribed countries are likely to be those most frequently identi-fied as 'threshold' or 'opaque' proliferators – such as Iraq, Libya, North Korea and Iran. Disagreement among the leading suppliers on limiting technology trade to these and other countries has added fur-ther discord to the planned new organisation. The new institution will not operate according to a consensus rule on transfer approvals. For items not on the 'super-core' list, national discretion will determine whether particular transfers go forward. As a result, no Cocom-like veto will exist for any of the members of the multilateral regime. Instead, prior consultation on *deliveries* of technologies of concern will be instituted in both the dual-use technology and munitions areas.[5] Interestingly, if these consultations develop as hoped, they will repre-sent a breakthrough beyond anything achieved in either the abortive P-5 arms transfer consultations of 1992, or the UN Arms Transfer Regis-ter.

The proposed organisation will be much less formal than Cocom. Rather than a supra-regime replacing institutions such as the MTCR and the Australia Group, the new organisation will have links with each of the major non-proliferation regimes – the MTCR, the Australia Group, the NSG and, importantly, accession to the NPT as criteria for membership. National export-control systems will also be required to meet minimum Cocom standards. This requirement will likely present serious near-term difficulties for countries in the former WTO. Most importantly, Russia – a founding member of the new organisation –

may not meet the rigorous requirements for strong export controls. Ensuring Russian participation is understood to be more important, however, than a narrow insistence on satisfying all the membership criteria. Yet this means that the new organisation will operate a weakened set of coordinated controls than existed under the old Cocom system. Assistance to states in the former Soviet Union and East-Central Europe in export controls administration was forthcoming in both the Cocom-coordination forum *and* the NATO Cooperation Council (NACC). These efforts will likely continue, as the export controls of these former adversaries come to constitute the weakest link in the redesigned Western framework of export controls.

Controls Initiatives in the European Union

In Europe, efforts to establish a common European policy on dual-use technology trade led to the drafting of a guideline by the European Commission in August 1992. This initiative includes:

- A broad-scope list of dual-use items, including most of those proscribed under the MTCR, the NSG and the Australia Group;
- Listed items would be subject to individual licensing, with a dedicated 'exclusion list', under which especially sensitive items would be subject to intra-European export licensing;
- A catch-all clause subjecting non-listed dual-use items to multilateral control when the supplier has knowledge, or has been informed by a government, that transferred items will be used in developing weapons of mass destruction and other military projects.

Even here, however, the 12 members of the European Union have been unable to reach agreement on a list of proscribed destinations – thereby duplicating the failure of the Cocom states to agree on this issue.[6] Proposals for a Europe-wide export-control agency also foundered on the objections of many countries to an expansion of Commission competence into the security area, most notably by France and the UK.

Article 223 of the Treaty of Rome significantly inhibits the activities of the European Commission in regulating dual-use technologies with many weapons applications. All 12 of the Union's members are, however, also members of the Australia Group and the MTCR. This means that common EU positions can evolve, although at present only through the expanded European Political Cooperation (EPC) mechanism designed to foster common foreign – and eventually defence – policies. This policy coordination is carried out on the periphery of the supplier groups themselves, however, and competes with bilateral diplomacy involving the United States and the other key Western states. The biggest change to the export control scene in Europe occurred on 1 January 1993. On that date the Single Market removed customs controls among the 12 members of the Union, thus creating potential problems in tracking the movement of sensitive dual-use items within Europe. In the trade of arms and nuclear goods, however, there is no longer the need to obtain International Import Certificates. Instead, firms need only file a copy of the freight document and/or a delivery declaration or bill with the recipient confirming acceptance of a transfer.[7] For dual-use items, firms must send a second copy of their export certificate to the Export Control Office (in the recipient state). No confirmation of receipt need be provided by the receiving party. It remains to be seen how dual-use firms will adapt their trade practices to the Single Market. It seems clear, however, that intra-European trade offers new opportunities for unscrupulous parties to divert sensitive technologies to the weakest regulatory destination in the Union. The pronounced variation in export-controls administration throughout Europe guarantees that criminal activity will continue in this area.

Notes

Chapter I

[1] Richard F. Grimmett, *Conventional Arms Transfers to the Third World, 1985–92* (Washington DC: Congressional Research Service, 19 July 1993), p. 50.

[2] Daniel Sneider, 'Lack of Funds May Stymie Russian Arms Development', *Defense News,* 31 January–6 February 1994, pp. 14 and 20.

[3] Daniel Sneider, 'Russian Arms Consortium Targets Export Market', *Defense News,* 12–18 July 1993, pp. 1 and 20.

[4] Philip Finnegan, 'Economic Lull Slows Gulf Nations Buying Spree', *Defense News,* 13–19 December 1993, p. 32.

[5] Grimmett, *Conventional Arms Transfers,* p. 52.

[6] Gerald Segal and David Mussington, 'Arming East Asia', *Jane's Intelligence Review,* December 1993, pp. 565–66.

[7] See David Mussington, *Arms Unbound: The Globalization of Defense Production,* CSIA Studies in International Security 4 (Cambridge, MA: Center for Science and International Affairs, forthcoming), Chapter 1. Technical standards in weapons design are preferentially articulated by the leading weapons-producing countries and consumed as product standards by arms recipients.

[8] SIPRI, *SIPRI Yearbook 1993: World Armaments and Disarmament* (Oxford: SIPRI/Oxford University Press, 1993), p. 466.

[9] *Ibid.,* pp. 454–55.

[10] Even here, however, agreement is less easy to achieve than in the past. The successor organisation to Cocom has yet to form, mainly due to the lack of agreement among its potential members on formally naming the target countries of technology restrictions. See David Mussington, 'Defense Exports Seek New Framework', *International Defense Review,* March 1994, pp. 23–25.

[11] Directorate of Intelligence, *The Defense Industries of the Newly Independent States of Eurasia* (Washington DC: Central Intelligence Agency, January 1993), p. 6.

[12] 'Russia to Boost Defense Exports', *Russia/CIS Intelligence Report,* 26 April 1994. Cited in *Arms Transfer News,* 6 May 1994, p. 8.

[13] Sneider, 'Russian Arms Consortium Targets Export Market', pp. 1 and 20.

[14] See Leyla Boulton and Paul Betts, 'Cooperation Lifts Russian Aero Industry', *Financial Times,* 30 March 1993.

[15] Directorate of Intelligence, *The Defense Industries,* p. 2.

[16] Christopher Foss, 'Ukrainian T-84 Joints Tank Export Push', *Jane's Defence Weekly,* 29 January 1994, p. 10.

[17] See, for example, 'US Imposes Penalties Over Russian-Indian Rocket Deal', *Arms Control Today,* May 1992.

[18] 'Argentine–Iraqi Technology Transfer Discussed', *Latin America Intelligence Report,* 30 August 1993.

[19] The US Air Force is currently seeking to sell 300 used F-16A/Bs, and to use the proceeds to purchase new F-16C/Ds. Thus, the link between export sales and domestic procurement is becoming more direct than ever. See Theresa Hitchens, 'US Air Force Fears Dearth of Strike Fighters', *Defense News,* 25 April–1 May 1994, p. 14; and 'DoD Reviews F-16 Sell-off Plan', *Arms Trade News,* April 1994.

[20] 'Marietta Demands Part of US Savings on Dynamics Deal', *International Herald Tribune,* 21 February 1994, p. 6.

[21] Mark Werfel, 'Forge a New Partnership', *Defense News,* 14–20 June 1993, p. 13.

[22] Jacques S. Gansler, 'Collaboration, Internationalization, and Security', in

Ethan Kapstein (ed.), *Global Arms Production: Policy Dilemmas for the 1990s* (London: University Press of America, 1992), p. 37.

[23] 'Washington Outlook', *Aviation Week and Space Technology*, 21 June 1993, p. 17.

[24] US Congress, Office of Technology Assessment, *Global Arms Trade,* OTA-ISC-460 (Washington DC: USGPO, June 1991), p. 73.

[25] Public ownership does not mean reticence in export promotion. See Giovanni de Briganti, 'French Await Huge Saudi Arms Buy', *Defense News,* 22–28 November 1993, p. 18.

[26] Ironically, recent French interest in returning defence firms to the private sector comes from exactly this rationale.

[27] William Walker and Philip Gummett, *Nationalism, Internationalism, and the European Defence Market*, Chaillot Paper 9 (Paris: WEU Institute for Security Studies, September 1993), p. 48.

[28] This number is calculated by comparing US federal government defence procurement, federal support of defence research and engineering, and foreign military sales with aggregate US manufacturing output.

[29] OTA, *Global Arms Trade,* p. 18.

[30] IISS, 'Defense Industry', *The Military Balance 1993–1994* (London: Brassey's for the IISS, 1993), p. 98.

[31] Governmental support for these firms is increasingly targeted at those that innovate in both areas. See John D. Morrocco, 'ARPA Blazes Trail on Defence Conversion', *Aviation Week and Space Technology,* 8 November 1993, p. 42.

[32] An example of these investment barriers was provided by the Bush Administration's objections to the sale of LTV's aerospace unit to Thomson-CSF of France. The deal was aborted when French government control of Thomson became an issue.

[33] See 'Malaysian Order Signals Russian Arms Export Breakthrough', *Interavia Aerospace Review,* August 1993, p. 41. It is alleged that India will provide maintenance and training for the planes once they are acquired.

[34] 'Taiwan Studies RJ Workshares', *Aviation Week and Space Technology,* 16 August 1993, p. 33.

[35] Edward J. Laurance, *The International Arms Trade* (New York: Lexington Books, 1992), p. 152.

[36] *SIPRI Yearbook 1993*, p. 477.

[37] This is an artifact of a broader technological convergence in the West. See Jacques S. Gansler, 'Managing Defense Technology: Problems and Needed Changes', in Asa A. Clark IV and John F. Lilley (eds), *Defense Technology* (New York: Praeger, 1989), p. 205.

[38] For an early example of this phenomenon, see 'Sale of F-16s Gets Initial Support', *Jane's Defence Weekly,* 12 February 1994.

[39] Martin Streetly, 'Making a Mark on a Mixed Market', *Jane's Defence Weekly,* 13 November 1993, pp. 25–30.

[40] 'UAE Seeks Offsets for Arms Buy', *Jane's Defence Weekly*, 12 February 1994.

[41] 'Offsets – Taking a Strategic View', *Jane's Defence Weekly,* 5 February 1994, pp. 23–30.

[42] See, for example, Malaysia's highly complex negotiations with Russia on technology transfer in its acquisition of 18 MiG-29 aircraft; 'Malaysia Seeks Business from MiG Deal with Russia', *Defense Marketing International,* 3 September 1993.

[43] United Nations, *United Nations Register of Conventional Arms, Report of the Secretary-General,* United Nations General Assembly, 48th Session, 11 October 1993.

[44] Malcolm Chalmers and Owen Greene, *The United Nations Register of Conventional Arms: An Initial Examination of the First Report* (Bradford:

Department of Peace Studies, Bradford University, October 1993), p. 7.
[45] Malcolm Chalmers and Owen Greene, *Background Information: An Analysis of Information Provided to the UN on Military Holdings and Procurement through National Production in the First Year of the Register of Conventional Arms,* Bradford Arms Register Studies no. 3 (Bradford: Department of Peace Studies, Bradford University, March 1994), p. 3.
[46] Ironically, the release of information following the Gulf War is greater because of the increased sales to Iraq's enemies. See Finnegan, 'Economic Lull', p. 32.
[47] 'Military Expenditure, Production and Trade 1992', *SIPRI Yearbook 1993,* p. 442.
[48] Chalmers and Greene, *The United Nations Register of Conventional Arms,* p. 11.
[49] Christopher Foss, 'Staying Strong Through Exports', *Jane's Defence Weekly,* 14 August 1993, pp. 22–23.
[50] 'Estonia Purchases Arms from Israel', *International Herald Tribune,* 25 May 1993.
[51] Barbara Opall, 'Upgrade Work Could Top New Sales', *Defense News,* 9–15 August 1993, p. 16.
[52] Andrew Lawler, 'US to Maintain Missile Export Control', *Defense News,* 13–19 September 1993, pp. 1 and 52.

Chapter II
[1] See Mussington, 'Defense Exports Seek New Framework', pp. 23–35.
[2] See Herbert Wulf, 'Switzerland', in Ian Anthony (ed.), *Arms Export Regulations* (Oxford: Oxford University Press, 1991), pp. 156–64.
[3] Ian Anthony, 'The Coordinating Committee on Multilateral Export Controls', in *ibid.,* pp. 207–11.
[4] Laurance, *The International Arms Trade,* p. 158.
[5] The old 'China Green Line' under Cocom saw China receive preferential

treatment on export controls in an attempt to drive a wedge between it and the Soviet Union.
[6] Peter Van Ham, *Managing Non-Proliferation Regimes in the 1990s: Power, Politics and Policies* (London: RIIA/Pinter, 1993), p. 20.
[7] Intellectual property-sharing within joint ventures may inadvertently violate security regulations. The higher the number of joint ventures, the greater the potential problem.
[8] Nancy Dunne, 'Ex-Soviet States Invited to Join New Cocom Body', *Financial Times,* 3 June 1992.
[9] 'A Call to Arms', *Flight International,* 10 February 1993, p. 3.
[10] Ioanna Iliopolus and William E. Hoehn, *Creating a New Export Control System: An Assessment of Congressional Proposals to Rewrite the Export Administration Act* (Washington DC: BENS, February 1994), p. 9.
[11] OTA, *Global Arms Trade,* pp. 101–2.
[12] *Ibid.,* p. 123.
[13] Laurance, *The International Arms Trade,* p. 131.
[14] David Mussington, *The Shape of US Counter-Proliferation Policy: From Prohibition to Stabilization and Management,* unpublished manuscript, 1993, p. 14.
[15] One potential source of technology is Ukraine. See 'Ukraine Agrees to Dismantle Arms', *International Herald Tribune,* 26 October 1993, p. 5.
[16] See 'Middle East Orders $35bn in Arms Since Invasion of Kuwait', *Financial Times,* 24 August 1992.
[17] Kenneth Timmerman, 'Look Who's Sending High-Tech Dynamite to Iran', *International Herald Tribune,* 25 October 1993, p. 4.
[18] South Africa, for example, is now well positioned to re-enter the arms market. See Philip Finnegan, 'South Africa Targets Exports', *Defense News,* 15–21 November 1993, pp. 1 and 28.
[19] Laurance, *The International Arms Trade,* p. 188.

[20] In spite of this possibility, other countries are imitating US defence technology investments. See OTA, *Global Arms Trade*, p. 41.

[21] Paolo Guerrieri, 'Technological and Trade Competition: The Changing Positions of the United States, Japan and Germany', in Martha Caldwell Harris and Gordon E. Moore (eds), *Linking Trade and Technology Policies* (Washing6ton DC: National Academy Press, 1992), p. 30.

[22] Philip Finnegan, 'European Companies Slow to Diversify', *Defense News*, 19–25 July 1993, p. 16.

[23] OTA, *Global Arms Trade*, p. 67.

[24] Giovanni de Briganti, 'Europe Targets Mergers to Bolster Industry', *Defense News*, 19–25 July, pp. 10 and 18.

[25] Laura D'Andrea Tyson, 'Managing Trade Conflict in High Technology Industries', in Harris and Moore (eds), *Linking Trade and Technology*, p. 74.

[26] Richard A. Cohen and Peter A. Wilson, *Superpowers in Economic Decline: US Strategy for the Transcentury Era* (New York: Taylor and Francis, 1990), pp. 113–14.

[27] Elizabeth Skons, 'Western Europe: Internationalization of the Arms Industry', in Herbert Wulf (ed), *Arms Industry Limited* (Oxford: Oxford University Press, 1993), p. 160.

[28] See George Leopold and Naoaki Usui, 'Mitsubishi to Transfer FSX Radar to US', *Defense News*, 14–20 June, 1993, pp. 3 and 58.

[29] Ian Anthony, 'The United States: Arms Exports and Implications for Arms Production', in Wulf (ed.), *Arms Industry Limited*, p. 79.

[30] Interview with US government official, May 1994.

[31] 'Congress to Move Quickly on EAA', *Export Control News*, 28 February 1994, p. 6.

[32] 'Comparison of Industry and Administration EAA Proposals – Key Provisions', *Export Control News*, 28 February 1994, p. 5.

[33] Continuing disagreements between the Administration and Congressional leaders meant that, as of early June 1994, US government officials were unwilling to hazard an estimate as to when the legislation would be submitted to the President for his signature.

[34] Laurance, *The International Arms Trade*, p. 179.

[35] Philip Finnegan, 'US Weapons in Gulf May Surge', *Defense News*, 22–28 November 1993, pp. 1 and 45.

[36] Philip Finnegan, 'Kuwait Eyes Russian, Chinese Arms', *Defense News*, 25 April–1 May, 1994, pp. 1 and 37.

[37] President Yeltsin signed Presidential Decree 507 on 5 May 1992. This set up an elaborate export-control framework, centred on the Ministry of the Economy (formerly Gosplan), and controlled by the Ministry of Foreign Affairs.

[38] Brendan McNally, 'Russians and Slovaks Swap Jets for Debt', *Defense News*, 22–28 November 1993, p. 36.

[39] Michael Klare, 'The Next Great Arms Race', *Foreign Affairs*, vol. 72, no. 3, Summer 1993, pp. 136–52.

[40] 'Sukhoi Fighter Family Grows', *International Defense Review*, August 1993, p. 608.

[41] Clifford Beal and Bill Sweetman, 'Beyond Sidewinder: Trends in Air-to-Air Missile Development', *International Defense Review*, January 1994, pp. 39–43.

[42] Opall, 'Upgrade Work Could Top New Sales', p. 16.

[43] More recently, France has entered the fray with a radar upgrade for the Russian MiG-21 jet. See Giovanni de Briganti, 'French Join Bid to Upgrade Russian-Built Fighters', *Defense News*, 21–27 February 1994, pp. 4 and 60.

[44] Lisa Burgess and Naoaki Usui, 'Japan Leads Quest for Asian Export Control', *Defense News*, 1–7 November 1993, pp. 1 and 36.

[45] Van Ham, *Managing Non-Prolifera-*

tion Regimes in the 1990s, p. 12.

[46] See Thomas Bernauer, *The Chemistry of Regime Formation* (Aldershot: Dartmouth/UNIDIR, 1993), p. 13.

[47] It is of course true that the fate of the Australia Group's special dual-use controls will determine whether this fortuitous situation continues. It is as yet unclear whether developing state signatories within the CWC will continue to be targeted by Australia Group restrictions.

Chapter III

[1] Jon B. Wolfsthal, 'Administration's Export Act Proposal Rankles Industry, Control Advocates', *Arms Control Today,* April 1994, p. 24.

[2] Again, Russia is unlikely to restrain its own sales in the face of increasing market domination by the United States.

[3] Philip Finnegan and Theresa Hitchens, 'Rewrite of Export Act Makes Odd Bed Fellows', *Defense News,* 21–17 March 1994, pp. 1 and 34.

[4] Of late, disagreement on the targeting of Iran as a dangerous potential proliferator is holding up the conclusion of negotiations. Russia, Germany and France are unwilling to 'name names' in a proscribed destinations list on the lines of the old Cocom model.

[5] This differentiation between opportunistic actors and more determined, non-status-quo states is developed by Janice Stein in an analysis of whether Iraqi leader Saddam Hussein could have been deterred prior to the invasion of Kuwait. The literature on proliferation control would profit from a more careful consideration of this issue. For a sensitive treatment of opportunism and non-status-quo actors, see Janice Stein, 'Deterrence and Compellence in the Gulf 1990–91: A Failed or Impossible Task?', *International Security*, vol. 17, no. 2, Autumn 1992, pp. 147–79.

[6] Interview with research analyst, Washington DC, May 1994.

[7] 'Offsets: Taking a Strategic View', *Jane's Defence Weekly,* 5 February 1994, p. 30.

[8] *Ibid.*

[9] 'UAE Seeks Offsets for Arms Buy', *Jane's Defence Weekly,* 15 February 1993. The Chairman of the UAE Offset Group, Amin Badr Al-Din, made clear that the UAE would refuse to sign any weapons contracts with defence contractors who refused to invest in the country.

[10] 'Malaysia Seeks Business from MiG deal with Russia', *Defense Marketing International,* 3 September 1993.

[11] 'Russia Sharpens Its Export Skills', *Jane's Defence Weekly,* 9 July 1994, pp. 28–29.

[12] While seemingly novel, this has already been achieved in the case of Saudi Arabia, the UAE, and supply relations with the UK and the US. See the discussion in Chapter I for details.

[13] See Ethan Kapstein, 'America's Arms Trade Monopoly', *Foreign Affairs* , vol. 73, no. 3, May/June 1994, pp. 13–19. While Kapstein seriously overstates the impact of US pre-eminence on global conditions, his emphasis upon continued US leadership is correct.

[14] The diminished credibility of Western promises of economic assistance removes more direct use of this policy tool from the current policy setting.

[15] Not all observers of defence industry trends feel that consolidation offers the potential for coordinated restraint. For an example of a different perspective, see Richard F. Grimmett, *Conventional Arms Transfers in the Post Cold War Era,* CRS Report for Congress (Washington DC: Congressional Research Service, 28 September 1993), p. 5.

[16] Interestingly, defence conversion programmes in the United States are over-subscribed (i.e., they have many more applicants than the funds available can support). One is left to wonder as to the potential for a multilateralised version of the US Technology Reinvest-

ment (TRP) programme that assists defence firms in developing products for the commercial market from defence (dual-use) technologies. See Gary J. Pagliano, *Defense Industry Transition: Issues and Options for Congress,* CRS Issue Brief (Washington DC: Congressional Research Service, 4 November 1993), p. 8.

[17] Such funds could be disbursed at either the central government or enterprise level, depending on policymakers' intentions. Assistance targeted at the enterprise level might speed the pace of industrial adjustment by giving a market valuation to the dual-use technologies contained there. This could be obtained through Russian participation in offset benefits competitions. Joint ventures between Russian and Western dual-use firms would further accelerate this process.

[18] Chalmers and Greene, *Background Information,* p. 70.

[19] *Ibid.,* p. 10.

[20] Israel is especially active in offering upgrades for weapons from the former Soviet Union. See 'Upgrading Russian Armour: The Israeli Experience', *Military Technology,* December 1993, pp. 66–68.

[21] One example is the integration of French radar equipment into upgrades of former Soviet aircraft. A number of joint-venture agreements have been signed between French aerospace companies and Russian defence enterprises toward this end. See Boulton and Betts, 'Cooperation Lifts Russian Aero Industry'.

Appendix

[1] Van Ham, *Managing Non-Proliferation Regimes,* p. 24.

[2] Variations in the enforcement of MTCR regulations are predictable, as are controversies over what constitutes a restricted technology. India's purchase of missile technology from France during the 1980s (inertial guidance assistance) provides a case in point, as does the involvement of German firms in the Condor II affair.

[3] Owen Greene, 'Successor to Cocom: Options and Dilemmas', *Safer World,* March 1994, p. 4.

[4] It remains to be seen how convincing developing states will find this argument in the context of the actual Treaty review. It seems likely that the issue will arise when consideration is given to indefinite extension of the Treaty, versus the option of extension for 15 or 25 years.

[5] It is anticipated that the International Munitions List from Cocom's controls will be retained almost unchanged. It remains to be seen whether the Atomic Energy List will be carried over to the new organisation. This particular regulatory structure may be transferred to the NSG for administration.

[6] Saferworld, *Briefing: Arms and Dual-use Export Controls: Priorities for the European Union* (London: Saferworld, June 1994), pp. 7–8.

[7] Harald Mueller, 'The Export Controls Debate in the "New" European Community', *Arms Control Today,* March 1993, p. 14.

Lightning Source UK Ltd.
Milton Keynes UK
UKOW06f1036100116

266081UK00002B/39/P

9 781857 531268